*TRAVELS IN MONGOLIA, 1902*

∞⧉∞

*uncovered editions*

Series editor: Tim Coates

Other titles in the series

*uncovered editions*

# TRAVELS IN MONGOLIA, 1902

## A JOURNEY BY C.W. CAMPBELL, THE BRITISH CONSUL IN CHINA

∞◦◦⋈◦◦∞

London: The Stationery Office

Applications for reproduction should be made in writing to
The Stationery Office Limited, St Crispins, Duke Street,
Norwich NR3 1PD

ISBN 0 11 702452 X

First published as Cd 1874, 1904
© Crown copyright

A CIP catalogue record for this book is available from the
British Library.

Cover photograph © The Royal Geographical Society,
London: Group of Kalmuchs outside their yurt. Photographers:
D. Carruthers and V.H. Miller, 1910–11.

Typeset by J&L Composition Ltd, Filey, North Yorkshire.

Printed in the United Kingdom for The Stationery Office by
Biddles Limited, Guildford, Surrey.
TJ978    C30    09/00

*Uncovered Editions* are historic official papers which have not previously been available in a popular form. The series has been created directly from the archive of The Stationery Office in London, and the books have been chosen for the quality of their story-telling. Some subjects are familiar, but others are less well known. Each is a moment of history.

*Series editor: Tim Coates*

*Tim Coates studied at University College, Oxford and at the University of Stirling. After working in the theatre for a number of years, he took up bookselling and became managing director, firstly of Sherratt and Hughes bookshops, and then of Waterstone's. He is known for his support for foreign literature, particularly from the Czech Republic. The idea for 'Uncovered Editions' came while searching through the bookshelves of his late father-in-law, Air Commodore Patrick Cave OBE. He is married to Bridget Cave, has two sons, and lives in London.*

*Tim Coates welcomes views and ideas on the Uncovered Editions series. He can be e-mailed at timcoatesbooks@yahoo.com*

*In the years following the 1900 Boxer Rebellion in China, there were several consular missions to remote parts of China and Mongolia. It isn't easy, from the reports, to understand what particular purpose was given to these expeditions, except to enlighten and enthral the members of the party. That in itself was sufficient to inspire some beautiful writing, with the apparent intention of conveying delight to the British Parliament.*

*On the journey described here, Consul Campbell travels north from Peking across the Great Wall and around the fringe of the Gobi Desert into Mongolia. On his route he describes the history, landscape and way of life of those he meets.*

*We have, for this edition, produced six new maps from the original map that Mr Campbell prepared for his report back to London.*

C. W. Campbell's route through Mongolia 1902

# AUTHOR'S NOTE

*The following notes are based mainly upon a journey undertaken last summer and autumn—June to October 1902—in Outer Chihli and Mongolia. Observations made in earlier excursions, and especially a diary of a summer trip to the Chahar country in 1899, are also drawn upon, but the dates are, I think, always mentioned.*

*Peking was my point of departure. As the reader can see from the map, it lies in the extreme north of the great Chihli plain, within a score of miles from the south edge of the Mongol escarpment. The new railway ends there, and though it is four or five days' march from the nearest territory inhabited by Mongols, there is no more convenient base for a journey to the plateau. To the Mongols there was much that was inexplicable in my apparently purposeless wanderings, but it seemed quite natural that I should come from Peking, which to them is the great city, the abode of the supreme mortal, the Emperor of China; and they have not yet completely forgotten that it was once the Tatu (Great Court) of Kublai Khan,★ and the seat of Mongol dominion for a century.*

**C. W. Campbell**
*His Majesty's Consul at Wuchow*

---

★ Kublai Khan, 1214–1294, first Mongol Emperor of China.

Peking to Dalai Nor

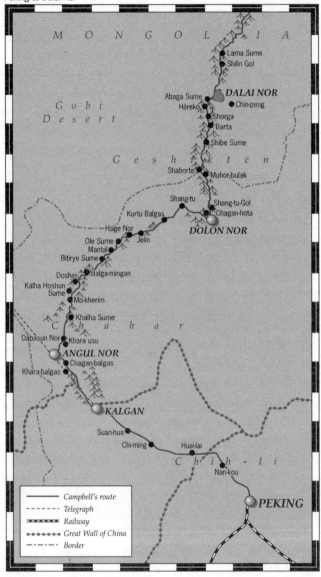

# PEKING TO KALGAN

In his first steps from Peking the traveller has a choice, if his carters will let him exercise it. The straight road northward to Nan-k'ou, on the verge of the Peking plain, passes through Ch'ing-ho (Clear River) and Sha-ho (Sand River); it is well known to tourists visiting the Great Wall and the Ming Tombs. A less direct, less beaten, but pleasanter route leads from the Tê-shêng Mên (Victory Gate) through Kuan-shih, and yielding to the solicitations of my carters, natives of Kuan-shih, who wished to spend one more night at home, I took that road on the 3rd June, 1902. It is necessary to be precise about dates, because the aspect of this plain varies enormously with the season. It was now in summer dress, a restful assortment of greens; but the heat was not yet of the monsoon, for which the farmers were longing. The country was parched. No rain had fallen for a fortnight, and the millet was bleaching. The roads, channels of dull ochre, were insufferable from dust; the pools had shrunk to patches of crust, and there was nothing to lay the impalpable powder, a blend of löss and alluvium, which the heated breeze kept in suspension.

A more populous plain than this it would be difficult to pitch upon. It is sown broadcast with villages, large and small, and so thickly that you are rarely a mile away from one. Each is marked by what looks like a copse from the distance, but is in reality a sparse sprinkling of willow, elm, pine, poplar, and pagoda (*Sophora*) trees, many of which shelter the tombs and cemeteries. The larger villages are ancient—trees and tradition say so—and the position of most is explained by the well, a perennial spring, soft and sweet in a plain where harsh alkaline waters abound. It is the core around which the primitive owners squatted thickly, exacting more elbow-room from later comers. An ugly little shrine in grey brick to Lung Wang (the Dragon Prince and God of Waters) stands sentinel over it; the heap of joss-stick ashes in the porthole opening upon the image bears witness—for this is not a people to burn incense to unserviceable gods—to his great reputation. The main highway, which a smart shower converts into a muddy ditch or a succession of brown pools, is the line of greatest length. The houses are dumped about irregularly, the richer protected by high brick enceintes [enclosures], the others by low mud walls or fences of sorghum stalks, and access to them lies often through winding lanes strewn with vegetable rubbish. There is rarely a pavement, and the absence of municipal control is inferred from the erratic encroachments of manure heaps and the numbers of seemingly ownerless beasts, mules, camels, or donkeys infesting the spare places; troops of children, naked except the older girls, cool brown unlaundered bodies in the shade; gaunt hairless camels—for they are now in summer coat—plod in file under loads of lime or coal; and dripping mules haul springless carts packed with grain or passengers. The side roads are few and noisome; the air throughout is weighted with human taints and the "smell of the East".

Wedged in between the villages, everywhere, there are countless cemeteries. Few families claiming respectability, no matter how poor, fail to keep a plot of ground set apart as a private graveyard, and the plain around Peking is also the burial ground of the city. Including the mausolea of princes and other magnates, which are enclosed by walls and fairly extensive, the spaces occupied by burial places must be enormous. Not so long ago it was held that they offered insuperable difficulties to enterprises such as railways, but public opinion, pressed by the economic necessities of a huge population, is rapidly making it less of a crime to utilize them.

In half-an-hour from the Tê-shêng Mên we passed through a cutting in the earth wall of Old Cambalue, and a few miles further on we struck the well-laid stone road which connects the Summer Palace with Peking, and bowled along it to the bourgade [village] of Hai-t'ien (Sea Field). The Western Hills were now close on our left hand: Wanshou Shan (Birthday Hill) in the forefront, still untenanted, though rumour had it that the Empress-Dowager longed to return to her favourite residence; on our right was Yüan-ming Yüan (Round Garden of Light), a waste of ruins, but none the less forbidden ground (a few years ago the Viceroy Li Hung-chang was reprimanded by Decree for visiting them casually in a sedan). Later in the afternoon we were abreast of Ta-chüeh Ssǔ, a Buddhist monastery of note at the foot of Miao-fêng Shan (Wonderful Peak), which is the highest of the hills bordering this part of the plain and the scene of annually recurring pilgrimages; a little to the north and on the slope of Miao-fêng Shan, a large tomb was prominent—that of the seventh Prince (seventh son of Tao-kuang and father of the present Emperor); and just over Kuan-shih was T'o-an Shan (Camel's Back Mount), a hill of renown easily recognizable from its name.

Kuan-shih is one of the many Mahommedan communities which are found dotted over North China; seven-tenths of the population, some 3,000, are *chieh chiao* (abstinence sect), the common name for Mussulmans [Muslims], who speak of the pure Chinese as *ta chiao* (great sect); and most of the seven-tenths bore the same surname, Li. My chief carter, a person of intelligence, averred that, according to the tradition handed down by the "old men" of the village, their forebears "came from the west" before the rise of the Ming dynasty.

I observed a new timidity in a section of the inhabitants which, I was told, dated from the events of 1900. Kuan-shih was well known as a centre of the carrying [transport] industry, and it was consequently one of the first places which the broken Chinese troops turned to in their flight northwards. It had also, by reason of this industry, an unusual proportion of well-to-do inhabitants, a class greatly affected by the fugitive warriors.

At Yang-fang, a little north of Kuan-shih, we left the foot of the hills, which curved westward, and cut a chord due north to Nan-k'ou, 8 miles distant, over a shingly plain, which in wet seasons is swept of much of its arable earth by torrential feeders of the Sha-ho. Somewhere between us and Ch'ang-p'ing Chou, a district town 6 miles to the east, Jinghis★ pitched his camp in AD 1211, after a long march from the Kerulon, and his son Ogotai did the same 20 years later in the course of the campaign which ended in the extinction of the Chin dynasty; and an hour's ride north of Ch'ang-p'ing Chou are the much-visited

★ Genghis Khan, 1162–1227, Mongol conqueror of northern China and Iran.

tombs of the Ming Emperors from Yung-lo down, known locally as the Shih San Ling (Thirteen Mausolea).

From Nan-k'ou (South Pass) to Kalgan there is but one road, a highway of immemorial reminiscence and writ large in Chinese annals. It was the principal line of irruption [invasion] of the turbulent nomads who, from the dawn of history to the establishment of the Manchu dynasty, periodically swept down from the wastes of High Asia, cut red lanes through the corn plains of North China, and reminded the peaceful farmers that there are scourges other than those of Heaven. Nan-k'ou itself is at the entrance to the defile [narrow pass] through the south line of the In-shan known as Kuan-kou (Government Defile)— a long, irregular street of inns and shops built over detritus and shingle; it has no commercial importance except as the first stage from Peking. For this purpose it fits in with the carrier's economy, for it is rather less than 30 miles from the An-ting (Peace) and Tê-shêng (Victory) gates and, under ordinary conditions of weather, a moderate day's march for cart or mule.

At Peking we were 120 feet above sea-level, at Kuan-shih 300 feet, and at Nan-k'ou 500 feet, but the ascent now became rapid, and 12 miles further on, close to the Inner Great Wall, the absolute altitude of the road was 2,100 feet. When I first made the acquaintance of the Nan-k'ou Pass in 1885, the highway had not been touched for a couple of centuries, and it was practically closed to wheeled traffic. About that time Li Hung-chang instituted a system of repair and maintenance, the financial basis of which was an impost [tax] on all passing vehicles, pack animals and cattle. A system of this sort seldom thrives for long in China, but in 1902 the excellent state of the road and the bands of workmen levelling and cutting it at two or three points showed that this one was still active and useful. The tax was insignificant—50 cash or 1½*d.* a cart; but my drivers, whose pay was 1,000 cash (2*s.* 6*d.*) a month and expenses (one of them told me that he had to support a family of nine on this), considered it a grievous burden, and lost no opportunity of saying so.

From Nan-k'ou to Chü-yung Kuan (950 feet above sea-level) the rocks were limestones, with intrusive seams of syenite and syenitic and granitic porphyries; at Chü-yung Kuan the highest of the hills hemming the defile are reached, and we pass beyond the limestones into a mass of granites veined with diorite and felsite. Chü-yung Kuan, "the foremost barrier under heaven" as an inscription over one of the gates informs us, appears in Chinese literature from the earliest times. Lieh Tzŭ speaks of it as a frontier bulwark, and he lived four centuries before Christ. The pass narrows, and there are fairly preserved walls still climbing the heights on either side which are said to have arrested the march of Jinghis, but the point of interest to the European traveller is the remarkable gateway called the Kuo-chieh T'a (the Pagoda bridging the Street). The name is explained by a tradition that at one time the arch supported a pagoda which was removed in the early years of the

Ming dynasty because Mongols could not be induced to pass under it. From one of the inscriptions on the walls of the arch we know that the structure was completed in AD 1345, and from another that it was repaired exactly a century later, in 1445. The first European to mention it is Gerbillon. In the journal of the first of his *Voyages en Tartarie* in 1688, he says:

> *Un de ces bourgs pourrait passer pour une petite ville (Chü-yung Kuan). La porte par laquelle on y entre ressemble assez à un arc de triomphe. Elle est toute de marbre et a environ 30 pieds d'épaisseur avec des figures en demi-relief jusqu'à la voûte.*
> [One of these villages could pass for a small town (Chü-yung Kuan). The gate by which you enter looks like an arc de triomphe. It is made of marble nearly 30 feet thick with carved figures as far as the arch.]

But he does not mention the inscriptions, and they remained unnoticed until Mr A. Wylie, who had read of them in a Chinese book on stone inscriptions, passed through the gate in 1863. The results of his researches were published in 1870 in the *Journal of the Asiatic Society*, and in 1895 facsimiles of the inscriptions were produced by Prince Roland Bonaparte in a magnificent folio. The arch is of white marble, the blocks being cut to form a ceiling of three plain surfaces on which Buddhistic figures are carved in relief. The walls of the archway from the spring [architectural term] downward are covered with similar carvings and with inscriptions in six languages, all of which are defaced and chipped, chiefly by the tremendous traffic through the gate. Five of these languages offered no special difficulty—Sanscrit (antique Devanagari), Chinese, Tibetan, Mongol, and Uigur—but the sixth was unknown; and although Mr Wylie adopted the view of a Chinese author, that it was Juchen (Neuchih, Nü-chen), the national script of the Chin or Gold dynasty, who followed the Kitans as the dominant power in North China in the early part of the twelfth century, it was soon remarked that the few known specimens of Juchen writing did not help this identification. It is only within the last few years that Dr S.W. Bushell, the physician at the British Legation at Peking, established that it is a Tangut script, of which few specimens are extant [still remain]. This writing was adopted in 1036 by Yüan Hao, the founder of the Tangut Kingdom, and it seems to have been "modelled on the lines of the antique Chinese official script called *Li-shu*." In those days a new dynasty meant not only a new name for the territory and a new seat of government, but also a new writing for official purposes. The Kitans, Juchens, and Tanguts were each specially provided with artificial scripts, which soon became extinct after the disappearance of the dynasties; specimens are now found only in a few stone inscriptions, coins, or courier badges, or in Chinese works on antique bronze and stone inscriptions. The Chü-yung Kuan archway and a stone stele [tablet] in a Buddhist monastery of Liang-chou in the Province of Kansu, called Ta-yün Ssŭ (Great Cloud Monastery), are the only two considerable examples of the Tangut script which are known to exist.

Light cooling zephyrs [breezes] mitigated the temperature in the pass, and as we emerged from the Great Wall through the *Pei Mên So Yüeh* (Lock and Key of the North Door), a bracing breeze smote through summer flannels to remind me that we had mounted the first step of the staircase from the Chihli plain to the plateau of Mongolia. The Huai-lai Valley entered at Ch'a-tao (Fork Roads), a tiny walled town of inns and rest-houses anciently called Pei-k'ou Chên (North Pass Borough), averages 1,600 feet above the sea, and this altitude deprives it of the privilege enjoyed by the Chihli plain of producing two crops in the year. Yet it is wonderfully fertile, especially in fruits—grapes, melons, apricots, persimmons (*Diospyros*), plums, pears, and apples—and the population, being less crowded, is less pinched by poverty.

The bread of this people is nothing more or less than polenta made of *hsiao-mi* ("little rice"), which is the local name of Italian millet (*Panicum italicum* L.). It is only the rich and the dwellers in large towns who eat rice. *Huang-mi* ("yellow rice"), a glutinous variety of millet, known to science as *P. miliacrum* L., is also known to a large extent. But the most striking grain of these parts is *Kao-liang* ("tall grain"), which I once heard a British infantry captain refer to as a "great grass". It is Pliny's millet, durra, Guinea corn, *Sorghum vulgare* Pers., and many other things, according to time and place. In tropical and sub-tropical regions it is as widely distributed as wheat in the temperate zones. In North China the seeds are ground and eaten in the form of cakes and puddings rather than bread, but most of the *Kao-liang* goes to feed the hard-worked mules and ponies, with whom it agrees better than any other local grain. The seeds are not the sole attraction. There is the long stalk, reaching to 16 feet in some varieties, which is put to a multitude of uses—fences, walls, and screens, and foundation thatches for clay roofs; the roots are dug up and are prominent as fuel; and the panicles are bound into brooms. Wheat, maize, and pulse are grown in quantity; oats and potatoes occur in the higher mountain valleys.

In the Huai-lai Valley our course is westerly, through Yü-lin-pu, Huai-lai Hsien, Tu-mu, Sha-ch'êng, and Hsin Pao-an to Chi-ming Yi. I noticed that the inhabitants, who never in my previous experience sought to be particularly friendly or unfriendly, were now elaborately civil in their attitude towards me and mine. My servants remarked more than once that the inn-people were studiously pleasant and moderate in their demands, and whenever I walked abroad, the smallest boys appeared to have been drilled into unusual habits of deference. At Sha-ch'êng I touched on the subject in a chat with an inn employee, and he assured me naïvely that the German expedition to Kalgan in the winter of 1900 was still a vivid memory. "Pu hao" (bad), he said, but the effects were so pleasant to myself that I could not wholly agree with him. "Civilization does get forrid [forward?] sometimes upon a powder cart."

Chi-ming Shan (Cock Crow Mountain) dominates the north-west angle of the Huai-lai Valley, and confines the Yang River in a narrow gorge, at the entrance to which, and close under the lee of the mountain, is the little fortress of Chi-ming Yi (Cock Crow Post). On the summit, which must be 1,500 to 2,000 feet above the plain, there is a Buddhist monastery, Yung-ning Ssŭ (Temple of Eternal Quiet), perched among the rocks, which was founded during the Liao dynasty, nine centuries ago. Gerbillon records that that most energetic of Emperors, Kang-hsi, climbed to it on the 19th October, 1696. I only know of one party of foreigners, Timkovski's, who have done so.

Turning the flank of the Chi-ming Shan, past some coal workings of no importance, we enter the gorge of the Yang River, and crawl along a narrow irregular track hewn rudely in the cliff side, of which I have seen rousing descriptions in the notes of previous travellers. It is no doubt the roughest portion of the Peking–Kalgan road, but the only danger arises from the impossibility of two carts passing each other except at a few favourable spots. Before engaging in a contracted section, the carters shout to warn teams coming from the opposite direction, but very often the warnings are unheard or unheeded, and the consequence is a block, which restless mules and heated tempers may make perilous. In three passages through the gorge I have suffered one block of half-an-hour which, but for the ingenuity of 30 or 40 carters in prizing long projecting axles over each other and readjusting loads, must have lasted half-a-day. There was less blasphemy than usual; passengers cooled themselves with spotless ice, which ragged youths dug out of the sands of the river—a common occupation in early June—and sold for 1*d*. a bucket.

The Yang-ho here winds north-westward, and we edge along it, passing the villages of Hsia and Shang Hua-yüan (Lower and Upper Garden—a Liao Emperor once cultivated flowers at Shang Hua-yüan), whose women offended the puritanical taste of my Chinese groom by appearing publicly in sleeveless jackets of greater covering capacity than many European dinner gowns. Palladius, in a diary, refers to the inhabitants of these parts as "Tartars" (he must have meant Manchus or *Mongols*), but the speech, physiognomy, and habits point to Shansi as the original home of these immigrants.

We leave the Yang-ho after Shang Hua-yüan, cross a redoubtable ridge called the Lao-lung-pei (Old Dragon's Back), drop to the river again at Hsiang-shui-p'u (Sound Water Cove), so named from the murmur of the shallows close by, mount another line of eminences, the Yao-êrh-liang, whence we descend gradually into the plain of Hsüan-hua.

In 1899 brigandage was rife in the Huai-lai and Hsüan-hua districts. At intervals of 2 miles along the route it had been found necessary to throw up guard-houses, white-washed mud cabins bearing ostentatious inscriptions designed to awe the evil-disposed, for the protection of wayfarers. They were supposed to be tenanted in hours of darkness by local police, but in practice they were always empty day or night, and the inscriptions alone kept the peace. I rode one day with a police inspector who was returning from an unsuccessful chase of highway thieves, and before reaching Hsüan-hua Fu, the prefectural city, we saw three heads slung in cages on poles by the road-side, on the spot where the owners of the heads had robbed a Mongol. There was nothing of the sort in 1902, and I entertained a weak suspicion that the German expedition to Kalgan, and the continued presence of foreign troops in Chihli, had something to do with the self-effacement of these freebooters. My police inspector was sure that they were a necessary evil. "They spring up like weeds," he said; "no sooner scotch one crop—there is only one punishment for them—immediate decapitation—than another arises." The foreign traveller, being curiously prone to resist with lethal weapons, unlike his Chinese congener [counterpart], who seldom ventures beyond a verbal defence, is almost immune from highway robbery.

Hsüan-hua Fu, known to Mongols as Bain Sume (Rich Monastery), the only city of consequence in the region between Peking and Kalgan, is over 1,000 years old. The walls, which were first faced with brick in 1440, are after the Peking pattern, and little inferior; they are 8 or 9 miles in circuit, and are pierced by seven gates. For ages the neighbourhood has been celebrated for "the great plenty of grapes and other kinds of fruit", which are conveyed cleverly to Peking in wicker crates and baskets slung on mules. A large proportion of the population is Mahommedan. Raschid mentions that many of the inhabitants of a city named Semali, which must have been situated in this valley, came from Samarkand, and planted orchards in the Samarkand style. I have been told on two occasions by Mahommedans (at Tien-tsin and Nan-k'ou), of markedly Turkish physiognomy, that they considered Hsüan-hua to be the earliest home of their forebears. North of the city there is a park of old trees, protected from the freshets [floods] of the Yang River by a low embankment. Dr Bushell says that in the thirteenth century it was the site for a short period of a residence of a Yüan Emperor under the name of "Chung-tu" (Mid Capital).

I was particularly struck by the numbers of pairs of boots hung in separate wooden cages in the arch-way of the main west gate of Hsüan-hua, the valedictory gifts of beneficent Prefects. It is an attractive custom in China to invite a departing Magistrate whose rule has been popular, to leave a pair of old boots for suspension in a prominent place as a hint to his successor to follow in his footsteps. It is a considerable honour to be asked to leave these boots, and the ruled make the request all the more eagerly because they believe in the efficacy of the hint. And it is indubitable that one either sees a lot of boots or none at all. The necessary popularity is usually acquired by keeping within certain recognized limits in the extraordinary demands on private purses which are so characteristic of Chinese administration.

On the 7th June I was roused at daybreak by the

impatient carters, and got off from the west suburbs of Hsüan-hua Fu on the stroke of 5. By 8.15 am Shih-huo tzu (Stone Gorge), a trachyte spur 500 feet above the level of Hsüan-hua (which has 2,000 feet of absolute height) was reached; an hour later we stopped to water the mules in Yü-lin (Elm Forest), a considerable village in a löss [sandy] dip; at 10.50 am we turned the 13 *li*★ temple, and shortly after noon I was settled in one of the many inns in the Shang-pu (Upper Quarter) of Kalgan, under the shadow of the Great Wall of China.

★ A Chinese unit of distance—about one-third of a mile.

# KALGAN

The student who turns to that mine of obsolete information, the last edition of the *Ta Ching Hui Tien* (Institutes of the Manchu Dynasty), published in the reign of Chia-ching, ascertains that there are five great post-roads from North China to Mongolia. Beginning from the east they cross the Great Wall at Hsi-fêng-k'ou (Joy Peak Pass), Ku-pei-k'ou (Old North Pass), Tu-shih-k'ou (Lone Rock Pass), and Chang-chia-k'ou (Chang Family Pass) in Chihli, and at Sha-hu-k'ou (Kill Tiger Pass) in Shansi. Chang-chia-k'ou, the route which we have been following, is better known to Europeans as Kalgan, a Russianized form of the Mongol name *Khalga* (the Gate).

Kalgan lies at the foot of the last ascent to the plateau, which here makes its nearest approach to Peking and the sea. It is a convenient market for a large part of South-East Mongolia, but it is pre-eminently a transport depôt, and owes its importance to the caravan trade with Urga and Uliasutai, Siberia, and Russia. Of the frontier trade centres it is inferior only to Kuei-hua-ch'êng or Kuku-hota, the Blue Town of Huc. There are three quarters: two south of the wall, called Shang-pu and Hsia-pu (Upper and Lower Citadel), of which the nuclei are two brick-walled fortresses of some antiquity, and Yüan-pao-shan (Ingot Hill), the north-west suburb, where the Russian merchants live. Gerbillon in 1688 dined with a rich merchant in Hsia-pu, of which he says, "*On y fait un gros commerce*" ["Business is good"], and no doubt for centuries before that the Mongols south of the Gobi found their way to Kalgan to barter horses and cattle for Chinese utensils and finery.

## HSIA-PU AND SHANG-PU: THE CHINESE AND MONGOL QUARTERS

The town may be said to begin at the T'ung-ch'iao (Through Bridge), a substantial stone structure which spans the Kalgan River at a point nearly 2 miles south of the Great Wall. This river, known locally as the

T'ung-ch'iao-ho, issues from a narrow gorge, the Gate, and flows a little west of south; the mountains take a more westerly curve from the Gate, and leave between them and the river an expanse of low, irregular slope, and it is on this that Kalgan is built. A few hundred yards west of the T'ung-ch'iao, outside and close to the south-east angle of the Lower Citadel (*pu-li-t'ou*), you enter the main business thoroughfare, which runs northward, and parallel with the river. Hsia-pu is considered the Chinese Kalgan. It does not depend exclusively on the Mongol trade, and nowadays it is not so much visited by Mongols; the firms catering for them find it more to their advantage to keep their places of business in the Shang-pu. Inside the Lower Citadel, which is an oblong of 750 yards by 450 yards, there are the Shansi banks and government offices, and grouped around them there is a large population interested in the carrying trade, in the preparation of hides and soda, in agriculture, and the hundred-and-one minor callings. Until you pass north of Hsia-pu the main street is typically Chinese—busy, lined on both sides with shops, and of fair breadth, but pedlars and street vendors spread their wares wherever they can snatch room, and the fairway for vehicles and horsemen is always narrow and congested. A sign of the comparative opulence of Chinese Kalgan is the number of temples, both inside Hsia-pu and out, the oldest of which is the Chên-wu Miao, a shrine in honour of Khabatu Khassar, the fighting brother of Jinghis.

Between Hsia-pu and Shang-pu the street, which is here called Wu-ch'eng Chiêh (Barrack Street), crosses a sandy water course, and passes west of the military cantonments and a large parade ground. Kalgan is officially a military post under the civil jurisdiction of Wan-ch'üan Hsien, a departmental city 10 miles to the west. For the past 200 years, since the days of Kanghsi, there has been a permanent garrison of varying strength, but in 1902 it was stronger than usual, and consisted of 1,100 troops of the Manchu Banner Organization. A new feature in the streets, a consequence of the German expedition, was a small body of police who wore neat blue uniforms and white sleeve-badges bearing the inscription "Police of Kalgan" in English and Chinese. North of the parade ground is the yamên [public office] of the Tu-t'ung, who is the Manchu Governor of the Chahars and other Mongol tribes.

From here you are in Shang-pu or Mongol Kalgan. There has been a gradual ascent, and the valley closes in rapidly, the walls of the gorge at the Great Wall being little more than a quarter of a mile apart. In this Shang-pu funnel, building ground is precious and every available inch is occupied. The main street is a continuation of that which you entered near the T'ung-ch'iao, though it bears another name, Ta-mên Chiêh (Main Gate Street), but it is narrower, and paved with stone blocks as a protection against the fierce traffic. Mongols are now common, lamas [priests], "black men" and weather-beaten wrinkled women, riding or trudging, rosary in hand or arm-in-arm, or chaffering [haggling] with eager Chinese, who all speak a mutilated Mongol. The shop floors stand above the level of the street, which becomes a stream in heavy rainstorms, and many are protected from inundation by a plank boarding slipped into grooves for the occasion. A caging of slender poles protects the windows and front of the shop, and is a survival common in the provincial towns of Outer Chihli of a period when property was less secure than it is now.

The Upper Citadel, a brick enceinte [enclosure] of smaller size than the Hsia-pu, is contiguous with the south face of the Great Wall where it crosses the gorge. It is known as the Shih-ch'üan (Market Enclosure). I found it in June a delightful little place—a quadrangle of trading establishments and temples, bright with oleanders, pomegranates, and roses (which the shopmen reared in pots), and ringing with the song of caged Mongol larks.

The Great Wall is passed by the Ta-ching Mên (Great Frontier Gate), which, in accordance with ancient custom, is closed at nightfall and opened at sunrise; and just outside it you notice, on the right hand, a considerable space raised some feet above the valley bed and bounded by a curved revetment [retaining wall] of rubble masonry. It is the horse and cattle market. Hither flock horse-dealers from as far south as Hunan, and ponies from Urga and the Kerulon. In June and July the horse trade is in full swing. Camels appear in the winter from November to February, and are bought for the Peking coal trade and for the Kiakhta tea caravans. Cattle and sheep are almost always for sale. Prices vary with the season and the condition of the market, but the average value of the pony is 20 taels★; of a bull or cow, 15 taels; of a good camel, 40 taels; and of a sheep, 1½ to 2 taels.

## FLOODING

The revetment I have mentioned is one of the features of Kalgan, and it requires only a slight examination to understand the reason for its existence. To the Kalgan gap the waters draining from some 2,000 square miles of the Mongol escarpment converge, and the quantities of eroded rocks and boulders cumbering the depths of the valley and the bed of the T'ung-ch'iao-ho suggest torrents of magnitude. Two ravines descend from the heights and join at the gap. The larger, from the north-east, is the post route, and is called the Chagan Tologai (White Head) Pass; the north-west ravine, the Barun Daba (West Pass) is the caravan road—shorter, narrower, and more precipitous. Smaller ravines and depressions run into these two, and they in turn have their branches, and so on, until the watershed is reached in minute folds and cuttings. The deciding rim averages 4,800 feet above the sea, and Kalgan is 2,700 feet; but the distance from the rim in places is scarcely over 12 miles,

★ The tael (ounce of silver) varies in weight and fineness with the locality; my sterling equivalents are approximations throughout.

and whenever a monsoon thunderstorm bursts over this ramification of ravines, the floods descend too rapidly for the capacity of the exit, the waters are banked up at the gap, and Kalgan barricades against inundation. The stone embankment is the first line of defence; it begins some distance up the Barun Daba, and is carried westward to the river and down the valley past the Upper Citadel. In early June there is no danger; the Chagan Tologai is almost dry, and there is but a trickle in the West Pass.

## THE TEA TRADE

Shops and timber yards continue westward up the Barun Daba, and Yüan-pao-shan (so named from its fancied resemblance to a shoe of sycee [silver ingot]) bounds the defile on the north. On the slope the houses of the Russian tea agents and the Russian post-office are terraced in a recess, all of them keeping a respectable height above the valley bed. In 1899 a niche in the bare rocks on the south side of the Barun Daba, opposite the Russian settlement, was occupied by a Greek church of slender size, but stately by contrast with the buildings in sight, and a genuine delight to the European eye. In 1902 it was in ruins—an eloquent testimony to Boxer violence.

Kalgan as a residence for foreigners dates from the early sixties [1860s], when firms interested in the tea trade took advantage of the special privileges conferred by the Russian treaty of 1860, and established agencies in Yüan-pao-shan to facilitate the transport of their teas across the Gobi to Urga and Kiakhta. Since 1865 Kalgan has been a prominent station of the American Board of Foreign Missionaries, and the occasional residence of English and Swedish missionaries, whose labours are specially directed towards the conversion of Mongols.

There were, in 1902, only half-a-dozen Russians in Kalgan and, except the Postmaster and the agent of the Russo-Chinese Bank, all were representatives of tea firms. The tea caravan traffic is diminishing rapidly, in consequence of the competition of the Manchurian Railway, assisted by the heavy duty lately imposed by the Russian Ministry of Finance on tea passing through Kiakhta, and very soon it must reach exiguous proportions. In the height of the trade over 300,000 chests of leaf and brick teas passed through Kalgan, and four-fifths of this trade was Russian. The tea came from Foochow and Hankow, by sea, to Tien-tsin; thence to Tungchou in Peiho river-boats; from Tungchou to Kalgan by camels or mules; and from Kalgan to Urga and Kiakhta by camels or ox-carts. The camel caravans took from 30 to 40 days (according to the amount of fodder along the route) to cover the 600 miles from Kalgan to Urga, and they always made the journey in autumn or winter. In good years camels could be depended on to accomplish two trips to and fro in the season; and as this means that one camel could only account for the carriage of eight chests, it is pretty evident that with the decline of the tea caravan a great incentive to camel-breeding in Mongolia will disappear.

The cost of transport of tea by camel from Kalgan to Urga averaged latterly 2½ taels (say, 6s. 6d. to 7s. 6d.) for a chest of 130 lbs.

In summer ox-carts come to Kalgan with salt, soda, and poles, and take away loads of tea to Urga and Kiakhta; but oxen require water and grass regularly, and the route must be adjusted accordingly. An ox-cart spends two—sometimes three—months on the road between Kalgan and Urga; however, in spite of the slowness, this mode of transport is cheaper than the camel caravan, and all the inferior grades of tea are entrusted to ox-trains. Before the construction of the Siberian Railway it cost 6d. a lb to carry the Russian tea by sea and caravan from Hankow to Moscow; I understand that, by Port Arthur and the railway, this 6d. has been reduced to 1d., and no doubt the rate can be brought lower still. The caravan tea spent six months on the road; the railway route takes, at present, one month.

## CUSTOMS REVENUE

Kalgan has a population of 70,000 or 80,000. There is a station of the Imperial Chinese Telegraph Administration, which is connected with the Siberian telegraphs by a line across the Gobi to Urga and Kiakhta. Kalgan is also a principal customs barrier for the taxation of Mongolian trade; inside the Ta-ching Mên there is a station with a glass window commanding a view of the gate and traffic, and as the droves and vehicles pass, the duties are assessed and levied by capable appraisers with commendable celerity [speed]. I was informed that the ordinary revenue accruing to the Chinese Government from the Superintendency was 50,000 taels. On looking through the old files of the *Peking Gazette* for statistics, I came across a memorial [report] of the Superintendent in 1879, and according to that, the Kalgan Customs were then rated at 60,561 taels a year; but there was a deficit of 20,256 taels, which he attributed to the tea trade having fallen into Russian hands and being thus freed from duty. His predecessors had usually been asked to pay only two-fifths of such deficits and, of course, he expected similar lenient treatment. My only comment on these figures is that of a Chinese merchant, who thought the post of Superintendent an agreeable appointment which a poor man might cheerfully accept, no matter what the condition of Mongol trade.

## CIVILITIES FROM LOCAL DIGNITARIES

Nearing the T'ung-ch'iao Bridge, on the 7th June, I was greeted by a guard of honour and the music of military trumpets, unexpected civilities resulting from private letters of recommendation which members of the Chinese Foreign Office had very kindly sent before me. But the summer costume of a civilian traveller who has just spent six hours on a dusty scorching road in North Chihli has nothing in common with military neatness, and I fear that incomplete justice was done to this, the one guard of honour of my life.

I had hardly arrived at the inn when a courteous Secretary, who spoke excellent English, called upon me on behalf of the Governor, and offered his services to expedite my journey, and soon after him came the Governor himself, the Deputy Governor, and the Superintendent of Customs. Invitations to dinners followed, and altogether I was treated with a *bonhomie* and friendliness which I had only once before experienced from provincial officials of rank. It is an old administrative rule to advance temporarily the grade of a Chinese officer sent on duty "beyond the passes", and I found that in the documents prepared for my use in Mongolia even this little attention was not forgotten and, by a dextrous rearrangement of the Chinese hieroglyphics used in my passport, I was invested with a title which my purse could ill support. I drew attention to this pleasant exaggeration, but the Secretary eluded my objections, said there were precedents, and that it was all for the best.

## *THE CHAHAR COUNTRY*

### KALGAN TO DOLON-NOR

The Peking mule-carts were discharged at Kalgan
and others were engaged to carry my baggage
over the rim of the plateau to a Mongol encampment at Khara-usu. Here I found a caravan of
camels, camel-cart, and ponies, which Mr A. Larsen,
a Swedish missionary of Kalgan, who joined forces
with me as far as the Kerulon, had very kindly

purchased for me beforehand, and with Mr Larsen's help it only took me a few days to make the final preparations.

## Angul Nor

Close by Khara-usu is Angul Nor, the largest sheet of water in the Chahar country. In 1899 I launched a duplex Berthon on this lake, the first boat seen in this part of Mongolia, and spent some days sounding it [measuring its depth] and collecting botanical and natural history specimens in the neighbourhood. Last year Chabeh Singh, a sub-surveyor, whose services were lent to me by the Indian Intelligence Department, made a sketch of it, which places its outlines on the map accurately for the first time. It is heart-shaped, the greatest length is 7 miles. I rowed across it from north to south, and found no greater depth than 4½ feet. Mr Larsen took a line east and west, and had an exactly similar experience. The average depth cannot be much over 2 feet. The water tastes strongly of soda, is charged with organic impurities, and quite unpotable; but the cattle and ponies seem to thrive on it, and the camels love it. A sample of this water, which I sent to the Health Officer of Shanghae, Dr Arthur Stanley, was pronounced by him to be "highly poisonous as a beverage" and destructive "of animal and most vegetable life." I spent some time in a fruitless search for fish, and finally came to the conclusion that there are none in the lake. There was nothing living in it except a few water-fleas and patches of a species of water-grass. The bottom throughout was blue mud, or ooze, which often stank. Swans—I counted over 80—and sheldrakes were breeding, and the Mongols said that they came every year.

The lake is merely a local area of depression dammed on the west and south by low hills, and fed by a few wet-weather streams from those hills, and by the Khara-usu River, which makes a circular sweep from the east, drains a considerable area, and enters the lake at its northernmost point. The Khara-usu River in July 1899 was a mere trickle of running water; in June 1902 it was a series of shallow pools. After many rains it swells to a width of 10 yards and is 2 to 3 feet deep. The nature of the east shore shows that a large expansion takes place in rainy seasons, and the Mongols told me that in droughts the lake is smaller than I have seen it.

The Berthon boat excited the interest of the local Mongols. Parties collected on the shore, and there was much speculation as to what would happen when it reached the middle of the lake. A huge water-ox who dwelt there was certain to resent intrusion, and if I escaped the ox I must infallibly disappear in the great centre hole which led into the bowels of the earth. There was, I believe, a sharp division of opinion about my proceedings: some thought them indicative of mere lunacy, but the more numerous section credited me with material designs. The local Prince was selling the freehold of the cultivable portions of his territory to Chinese at the rate of 4 or 5 ounces of silver (say, 12*s*. to 15*s*.) the acre, and as cultivated land was permanently withdrawn from the common pastures and, moreover, gave rise to complaints of trespass, all such transactions were the subject of wide discussion and some popular feeling.

## Khara-balgas and Chagan-balgas

There are between Kalgan and Angul Nor the remains of two walled cities, the first of which, Khara-balgas (Black City), dates probably from the Liao dynasty. In the Mongol period it received the name of Hsing-ho-ch'êng, by which it is known to the Chinese at the present day. Till recently it was like all these ancient cities of Mongolia—uninhabited; in 1872 Dr Bushell remarked that it was "completely deserted and overgrown with grass", but about 15 years ago Chinese farmers started cultivating the space enclosed by the walls, and in 1899 there was a flourishing Chinese temple and a Chinese village of 40 or 50 houses occupying the centre of it. A fair held yearly towards the end of July is one of the events of the Mongol border. The earth walls, long flattened by the elements into mounds of gentle outline and grass-covered, face the points of the compass, and are half-a-mile square. They must have been 30 feet high originally, and there are traces of a 40-foot ditch running outside them, the water for which came from the Borochei rivulet close by. The north-west angle of the wall is surmounted by a small Chinese shrine built up against an ancient Mongol *obo*, or prayer-cairn, and during the fair of July 1899 I saw hundreds of Chinese worship at the shrine, and but few Mongols pay any mark of respect to the *obo*.

Some 8 miles north-west of Khara-balgas is Chagan-balgas (White Wall), which has been identified with Marco Polo's Chagan Nor. It is smaller than Khara-balgas, the space enclosed is 600 yards square, but the corners of the walls and the gates, of which there appear to have been four, were faced with brick. Towards the centre there was in 1899 a large oblong heap composed of broken bricks and building rubbish, amongst which I noticed pieces of the green and yellow tiles distinctive of Imperial buildings. There were traces of an exterior wall some distance outside the city. No doubt Chagan-balgas was one of Kublai's hunting or summer residences. I saw nothing of the "circular place enclosed by unhewn stones" mentioned by Timkovski, who visited Chagan-balgas in 1820. Some 20 Chinese families live under the lee of the north wall, and they have dug the bricks for their houses out of the corners and gateways. Three-fourths of the interior space is under cultivation. This is quite recent; the Chinese told me that they came four or five years previously, but Mr Larsen, who visited the place in 1895, was certain that it was then uninhabited and uncultivated. I saw later on, in the keeping of the Roman Catholic Mission near Hsing-ho-ch'êng, a dragon's head in marble and one or two other relics of Chagan-balgas, but nothing bearing an inscription.

## Chinese immigration

The Great Wall which we passed at Kalgan has long ceased to fulfil the last of its functions, that of a political boundary. The expression K'ou-wai (Beyond the Passes) applied to the region outside the Wall, can no longer be taken as a synonym for Mongolia. As the pressure of population in Shansi and Chihli increased, swarms of Chinese spread beyond it, ousting the Mongols, and gradually colonizing all the mountains which form the broad staircase to the high plains inland. Already the line of advance encroaches seriously on the plains. I had an opportunity of judging the speed of this invasion. In 1899 the Chinese settlers had reached a mile or so beyond Chagan-balgas; in 1902 I found them ploughing the virgin turf near Dabasun Nor, a pool which is 10 miles further north. All these Chinese settlements, which extend along the edge of the plateau from the Yellow River to the Hingan Mountains, are withheld from Mongol jurisdiction. They are governed by special Prefects, three of whom are stationed at Kalgan, Tu-shih-k'ou, and Dolon-nor.

## Mission at Hsing-ho-ch'êng

At the end of July 1899 I spent a day at the *chrétienté* [Christendom] of Hsing-ho-ch'êng, some 10 miles from the ancient Khara-balgas. It was founded in about 1880 by the purchase of a 2,000-acre block of arable ground, for which the Belgian Mission of

Eastern Mongolia paid 3,000 taels. The land is poor, sandy or gravelly in places, and on some of it I noticed encrustations of soda; but it supported 100 Chinese families of 700 souls comfortably. These families were mostly Roman Catholic converts from congested communities south of the Great Wall, and they tilled the mission land on the *métayer** system, surrendering 10 per cent to 30 per cent of the produce, according to the yield. I was informed that the Mission's title was registered officially in Peking, and that a yearly land tax of 130 taels was paid to the Manchu Governor of the Chahars.

The Mission revenue averaged 500 piculs[†] of grain (30 tons), worth 2,000 taels, but in bad years much of this was returned to the poorer cultivators in food and clothing. Disputes in the community were decided by the priest in charge (usually a foreigner, Belgian or Flemish, though in 1899 a clever Chinese seminarist was the pastor), who enforced the discipline of the Church. For instance, all members of the Mission were expected to say their prayers twice a day, and a persistent refusal to conform to this and other rules of conduct led to expulsion.

There are many similar *chrétientés* on the Mongol border from the Hingan Mountains to Kansuh, under the sway of four bishops of this Mission, and all are practically self-supporting. The Chapel at Hsing-ho-

---

* A farmer who pays rent by a fixed proportion of the crops.

[†] A Chinese weight of about 60 kg.

ch'êng was a brick structure with a roof of corrugated iron, which was rendered additionally conspicuous in this treeless upland by a copse of poplars, elms, and willows. The missionaries had planted these trees and carefully fostered them. Father Fan told me that as saplings they had to be protected from the fierce spring gales by mud walls, and in dry seasons watering was still necessary. There was an attempt at a flower garden—a few dust-covered marigolds and balsams, and a sickly rose bush trained under the lee of a wall.

## Political divisions of Mongolia

While on the threshold of Mongolia it will, I think, make my description a little clearer if I outline as briefly as possible the political geography of this part of the world. The Chinese Government recognize two Mongolias, Nei Mêng-ku (Inner Mongolia) and Wai Mêng-ku (Outer Mongolia), which are divided roughly by a line drawn in a north-easterly direction through the centre of the Gobi Desert. Inner Mongolia lies to the south and east, and extends over the plateau beyond the Hingan Mountains into the upper valleys of the Manchurian rivers, the Liao and the Sungari; it is peopled by the 24 tribes of the Inner Mongols, who are divided for administrative purposes into 49 Hoshun (whence a common designation of the Inner Mongols), by the eight Chahar banners (an imitation of the Manchu Banner Organization of Peking, and equally decadent), and the herdsmen of the Imperial Pastures. Outer Mongolia stretches along the Siberian frontier from near Lake Kulun to the Altai, and includes the four Aimaks or Khanates of the Khalhas, and the west Mongol territories under the jurisdiction of the Chinese Military Governor at Uliasatai-Kobdo, Tarbagatai, and Uriankhai. In the term Outer Mongolia may also be included the Mongols of Kokonor and Tsaidam, who are under the control of an Imperial Agent stationed at Hsi-ning Fu.

The Mongolias are excrescences [outgrowths] in the Chinese system of government. The regular administration is confined to the Shih Pa Sheng (Eighteen Provinces of China Proper); Manchuria, known as the Tung San Sheng (Three East Provinces) is in normal times under a separate organization of its own, officered almost wholly by Manchus; and the rest of the huge fabric—Tibet, Ili, Uliasutai, Kobdo, Kokonor, and the Mongolias—is held together by residents of sorts, chiefly Manchus of high rank, who are under the control of a Board at Peking, called the Li Fan Yüan (Court for the Regulation of Feudatories).

### Khara-usu to Shangtu

On the 16th June, 1902, we set out from Khara-usu (Black Water), and took a north-easterly course through a Khalha *hoshun* (banner) of the Inner Mongols and the territory of two Chahar banners and the Imperial Horse Pastures, to the ancient summer seat of the Yüan Emperors, Shangtu. We made a detour to avoid the direct route to Dolon-nor, which we wished to stop at eventually, to renew our stock of flour and millet, and the greater part of our route was new. Till we reached the Shangtu Gol there was no running water. Pools and lakelets, every one of which has a name—Dabasun Nor (Salt Lake), Hatate Nor (Stone Lake), Chamin Nor (Way Lake), Hagiye Nor—abounded: all permanent or semi-permanent sheets of water, no matter what the size, are called *nor* alike by the Mongols. There were occa-sional stretches of a steppe which rolled into the horizon, but as a rule our view was bounded by low green hills of soft outlines. Plain and hill were treeless: I saw only two or three stunted elms in sheltered clefts. Except in the Shangtu Valley, the Mongol tents were sparse, although the pasture was everywhere excellent, and the cattle and horses in thriving condi-tion. In a day's march, covering a view of 80 or 100 square miles, I could count 50 or 60 tents, say 40 fam-ilies, or something under two persons per square mile.

From Khara-usu to the Shangtu Valley the only permanent buildings were monasteries—Khalha Sume, Khalha Hoshun Sume, Bitirye Sume, and Ole Sume. At Mo-kherim (Bad Wall) we passed close to an earthen rampart, grass-grown, which I was told extended westward past the Kalgan–Urga route. From its antique appearance I judged it to be a Chinese defence of the pre-Mongol period.

On the 24th June we camped in the south-east angle of a deserted walled town which is marked on

Waeber's map as Kurtu Balgasu. The Mongols living near call it Balgas simply, and know nothing of Kurtu-balgas; the Chinese name is Hsin-liang-ch'êng. The walls appear to have been constructed of earth only, and are now melted into a succession of grass mounds. They enclose a square of 1,300 yards and face 10° west of the magnetic north.

Near the centre of the enclosure there are the remains of substantial buildings, broken bricks and tiles, and a few weather-worn remnants of cut stone, but the bulk of the interior is covered with mole-hills and green sward which bear no traces of former habitations. Wang Yün, a Chinese traveller quoted by Dr Bushell, who went in the suite of Kublai to Shangtu in about AD 1260, mentions "the new city of Huan-chou" as being 45 *li* from Shangtu. The odometer [instrument for measuring distance] attached to my camel cart made the distance 12¾ miles, and the local Mongols called it 40 *li*. There is no other *balgas* [walled city] which so clearly represents Wang Yün's Huan-chou. Dondo-hota (Middle Town), a collection of 30 Mongol families clustered around a large Chinese dwelling, lies a mile to the south of Hsin-liang-ch'êng. I noticed here and elsewhere in the Shangtu Valley that many Mongol tents were protected from north winds by fences of boughs roughly plastered with mud.

I spent the afternoon of the 25th June inspecting the remains of Shangtu (Upper Capital) or, as the Mongols now call it, Cho Naiman Sume (The Hundred and Eight Temples). In the diary of his

*Troisième Voyage en Tartarie*, Gerbillon, under the date of the 19th May, 1691, mentions

> *la ville de Chantou, où les Empereurs de la famille des Yuans tenoient leur Cour durant l'été; où on voit encore les restes* [the town of Chantou, where the Yuan Emperors hold court during the summer, where you can still see the remains]

but the first description of these ruins was given in a paper by Dr Bushell, read before the Royal Geographical Society in 1874. I have nothing of importance to add to Dr Bushell's description. Since his visit some vandal lamas [Buddhist priests] have collected most of the interesting marbles and stone work and made an *obo* [prayer cairn] of them. The archway of one of the main gates, under which Kublai himself must have passed frequently, is still standing, but I saw signs that the ruins were being drawn upon for building materials, and as soon as the line of Chinese immigration invades this part of the Shangtu Valley, the disappearance of these interesting relics will be a matter of a very few years.

### Shangtu to Dolon-nor

From Shangtu to Dolon-nor is a short day's journey—under 20 miles—south-west over a succession of low hills. Dolon-nor (Seven Lakes), called Lama-miao (Lama Temple) by the Chinese, is the third of the great trade centres in south-east Mongolia. (On two Russian maps I have seen the Mongol name supported by seven minute lakes; but, as a matter of fact, these do not now exist.) It was the scene of the submission of the Khalha Princes to the Emperor Kang-hsi in 1691, a ceremony which Gerbillon, an eye-witness, describes in minute detail. My camp was pitched to the north-west of the town, on some rising ground between two extensive lama monasteries. One of these, Hui Tsung Ssǔ (Temple of the Gathering of the Clans) or, as the Mongols call it, Shara Sume (Yellow Temple), was erected in commemoration of the ceremony by contributions from the Mongol Princes assembled to do homage; and soon after its foundation Chinese traders were allowed to establish themselves a short distance off, across the Êrstêng Gol (a branch of the Shangtu River), and commence the Mai-mai-chên, or trade borough, which can now boast of 30,000 inhabitants. The other monastery, Shan-yin Ssǔ (Good Cause Temple) or Kuku Sume (Blue Temple), was built with a donation of 100,000 ounces of silver from the Emperor Yung-chêng, Kang-hsi's son, and contains a stone memorial tablet dating from the ninth year of his reign (1732).

## DOLON-NOR TO DALAI NOR

### Town of Dolon-nor

The town of Dolon-nor lies on a sharp bend formed by the junction of the Êrstêng Gol and another tributary of the Shangtu Gol, which is one of the upper feeders of the Lan River. It covers a space of a mile in length by 600 yards wide, the long axis being south-west and north-east. The population is now estimated at 30,000, but I doubt that it is so great. The habitations are not crowded, and the streets in June were never busy or thronged. The yamên of the local military authority (Chên-t'ai) and of the Prefect, Fu-min-fu, a civil officer who exercises jurisdiction under the authority of the Tao-tai at Hsüan-hua Fu, are in the north of the town, and close by them is the market place. In the south quarter a number of religious edifices of modern appearance—San Kuan Miao (Temple of the Three Officers), Ch'êng Huang Miao (Temple of the City Tutelary), Shan Shên Miao (Hill God Temple), and others—towered over the low roofs, and in front of some of them were *Hsi-t'ai* or stages, for the theatrical performances of which the peasant of Outer Chihli is so fond.

The town is divided into wards or compartments by stout wooden gates, and these were regularly closed at night as a precaution against robbery, which was much too common. The inhabitants generally appeared to be ill-fed and indigent [poor], and I concluded that life is harder in Dolon-nor than in the settlements to the south-west towards Kalgan. The majority of the shops dealt exclusively in skins, pelts, and wools, and in articles required by Mongols—saddlery, Mongol hats and boots, felt, tents, furniture and cabinets, copper and brass Buddhas, rude hardware, glass and agate snuff-bottles, pipes, and miscellaneous stores. It gladdened the eye in this grey waste to see east and south-west of the town a number of vegetable gardens protected by lines of willows, in which spinach, onions and garlic, radishes and Shantung cabbage were sedulously [diligently] cultivated.

## Ruins of Chagan-hota and Mongol superstitions

My first march from Dolon-nor was directed to the ruins called Chagan-hota (White Town). They are just under 7 miles by road to the north of the two monasteries. The outside walls of what was probably an imperial residence of Kublai's, of the same character as the Chagan-balgas near Angul Nor, enclose a space 350 yards square. They are still standing in parts; the north-west angle is intact, and shows that the walls must have been 20 feet high. They were composed of two facings of rubble packed with earth, and they taper from a breadth of 15 feet at the base to 5 or 6 feet at the top. The rubble is of smallish flat stones laid in lime mortar. There were evidently three gates, on the east, west, and south. A hundred yards north-east of the main enclosure there are traces of a smaller one, 80 yards by 70. Chagan-hota contained few buildings. There is one large mound near the centre, four smaller ones north of it, and two—evidently remains of pavilions—at equal distances south and south-west of it. No one lives in Chagan-hota, and my Mongol followers did not relish the prospect of camping inside it, as we did for two nights. The

Mongols believe that all these old palaces and cities are haunted, and that the spirits are prone to bring misfortune on intruders. It seems to be an equal article of belief that gold and valuables are to be found in all ruins, but delving is tabooed, because it would infallibly involve the neighbourhood in disaster—murrain [crop blight], drought, or plague.

North of the Shangtu Gol we entered a region of sand hillocks, which continued as far as the south shore of the Dalai Nor. According to Przhvalsky, the local designation of this region is Guchen Gurben (Thirty-three), but I was unable to obtain any confirmation of the name. The Chinese call it popularly the Sha-wo-tzŭ (Sand Nests). There is little or no population until Shibĕ Sume is passed. During more than one 24 hours we did not see a soul, and this was attributed by Mongols and Chinese alike to the prevalence of robbers, who find it perfectly easy to escape with stolen cattle or horses in this labyrinth of monticules [little hills]. There was a bewildering choice of cart tracks and paths, made by Chinese in search of the brushwood and sparse timber growing on the north slopes of the hillocks (few of them were over 100 feet high), and we strayed daily. A little north of Hsi-pei-miao (North-west Temple) or Shibĕ Sume we passed from the Chahar country (Gul-Kuku, or Plain Blue Banner) into the Geshikten hoshun of the Inner Mongols.

## ORGANIZATION OF THE CHAHARS

The existing organization of the Chahars dates from the foundation of the Manchu dynasty in the seventeenth century. The original Mongol inhabitants were moved elsewhere, and a mixture of tribes—Barhuts, Solonguts, Merkits, and Sumits amongst others, according to Pozdnyéev—were settled in their place, and formed into a banner corps after the Manchu model to act as a frontier guard. Unlike the other Inner Mongol tribes, the Chahars have no hereditary Princes or Jassaks. The chief control is in the hands of the Manchu *Tu-T'ung* (Lieutenant-Governor), whose seat is at Kalgan, and the local *noyon* (officials) are selected from the Chahars themselves, merit of some sort being the ostensible criterion. Educational tests are applied, and to give aspirants for office opportunities of acquiring the necessary knowledge of Mongol writing, there are public schools in each of the eight hoshun.

A large proportion of the Chahars are in Government pay, either as simple members of the banner corps, or as employees of the imperial stud and cattle farms, or in the post-road stages. A banner-man is supposed to receive 2 ounces of silver a month and rations of grain, in return for which he should undergo a short period of yearly training, and keep ponies and arms (officially the arms are still bows and arrows) in readiness for active service. The Chahar cavalry were summoned to the China wars of 1842 and 1860, but the force has no military value in its existing form.

It is a natural consequence of their dependence on the Chinese Government, and of the Chinese being next-door neighbours, that the Chahars are more sophisticated than other Mongol tribes. There is less of the nomad about them. Chahar notables who can afford them live in permanent houses of Chinese type (*baishin*), and to a large extent wear Chinese clothes and eat Chinese food. I think it is Hyacinthe who spoke of the Chahars nearly a century ago as "impudent, audacious, and thievish", and there is no doubt that the other Mongols give them a bad name at the present day for cattle-lifting and general dishonesty.

## WEATHER NOTES, JULY 1899 AND JUNE 1902

The following weather notes are based on a meteorological journal which I kept carefully from the 27th June to the 9th August 1899, during a trip from Peking to the Chahar country:

The temperature in the Peking plain ranged from 92 degrees Fahrenheit at 2 pm on the 26th June (Wan-shou-shan) to 77.6 degrees at 7 am on the 27th June (Kuan-shih). At Nan-k'ou the mean temperature on the 28th June was reduced to 72.1 degrees by a steady monsoon drizzle. In the Huai-lai Valley the thermometer ranged from 97 degrees in the afternoon of the 29th June (Sha-ch'êng) to 71.5 degrees at 5 am on the 30th June (Sha-ch'êng), the diurnal mean being 82 degrees on the 29th June and 80.6 degrees on the 30th June. On my return journey through this valley the daily mean was 79.7 degrees (8th August) and 80.3 degrees (9th August).

The mean temperature in the narrow Shang-pu gorge of Kalgan on the 2nd July, a clear, almost breezeless day, was just over 80 degrees.

It rained on three out of the six days spent between Peking and Kalgan (a thunderstorm on the 28th June), and there was usually a slight breeze from north-west or south-east.

The observations recorded in 1899 in the following tables were taken at Khara-usu (4,100 feet) and

### KHARA-USU, altitude 4,100 feet

| Date (1899) | Temperature | | |
|---|---|---|---|
| | 7 am | 2 pm | 9 pm |
| | Degrees F | Degrees F | Degrees F |
| July 5 | 60.3 | | 60.8 |
| 6 | 64.7 | 81.4 | — |
| 7 | 62.2 | 66.5 | — |
| 8 | 60.3 | 69.3 | 62.2 |
| 9 | 59.5 | 62.2 | 61.7 |
| 10 | 60.4 | 73.6 | 62.1 |
| 11 | 62.8 | — | — |
| 19 | 73.1 | 84.1 | 72.6 |
| 20 | 64.8 | — | 60.4 |
| 22 | 71.3 | — | 64.5 |
| 23 | 51.9 | 68.4 | 53.3 |
| 24 | 58.7 | 73.2 | 59 |
| 25 | 58 | — | 59.6 |
| 26 | 58.7 | 79.2 | 69.2 |
| 27 | 53.6 | 57.5 | 59.4 |

## Orto-bulak, Angul Nor, altitude 4,000 feet

|  | Temperature | | |
|---|---|---|---|
| Date (1899) | 7 am | 2 pm | 9 pm |
|  | Degrees F | Degrees F | Degrees F |
| July 11 | — | 76.8 | 64.2 |
| 12 | 64.3 | 76.3 | 64.5 |
| 13 | 58 | 78 | 67.2 |

## Erightu, Angul Nor, altitude 4,000 feet

|  | Temperature | | |
|---|---|---|---|
| Date (1899) | 7 am | 2 pm | 9 pm |
|  | Degrees F | Degrees F | Degrees F |
| July 16 | 62 | 88.8 | 75.8 |
| 17 | 66.8 | — | 68.6 |
| 18 | 67.8 | 76.8 | — |

in the neighbourhood of Angul Nor, and will give some idea of the July temperature on the south-east edge of the Mongolian plateau.

During the month of July 1899 I registered rain on 13 days, on four of which thunderstorms occurred (I counted ten storms on the 7th July at Khara-usu). The winds, which were usually "light", boxed the compass; the most constant breezes were from south-west and north-west.

In 1902 further temperature observations were taken in the Chahar country from Khara-usu to Dolon-nor (Lama Miao). They are also recorded in a table.

| Name of place | Date (1902) | Temperature (degrees F) | | | Remarks |
|---|---|---|---|---|---|
| | | 7 am | 2 pm | 9 pm | |
| Khara-usu | June 14 | 52.6 | 69.5 | 50.3 | |
| | 15 | 52.7 | 75.2 | 62 | Water, fresh from well 39.8° |
| | 16 | 61 | — | — | Water, fresh from well 39.2° |
| Dabasun Nor | 16 | — | 54.5 | 53.6 | Rain, slight |
| | 17 | 57.9 | 71.2 | 51.4 | |
| | 18 | 57.5 | — | — | |
| Khalha Sume | 18 | — | 81.3 | — | |
| Mo-kherim | 18 | — | — | 62.5 | |
| | 19 | 62.7 | — | — | |
| Doshe | 19 | — | 59.5 | — | Rain (thunder-storm) at Doshe |
| Baga-mingan | 19 | — | — | 54.2 | |
| | 20 | 55.2 | — | — | Rain |
| Mantal | 20 | — | — | 51 | Rain |
| | 21 | 56 | — | — | Rain, 4/100 inch in two hours |
| Hage Nor | 21 | — | 65.5 | — | |
| Jelin | 21 | — | — | 50.5 | |
| | 22 | 54.5 | 67.4 | 57.1 | |
| | 23 | 56.4 | — | — | |
| Huchir | 23 | — | 68 | — | Rain, heavy shower |
| Kurtu-balgas | 23 | — | — | 51.2 | |
| | 24 | 58.3 | — | — | |
| Shangtu | 24 | — | 71.3 | — | |
| Dolon Nor | 25 | — | 53 | 50 | Rain, slight |
| | 26 | 49 | 66.2 | — | Rain, slight |
| | 27 | — | 73.2 | 56.8 | Rain, slight |
| | 28 | 64 | — | — | Rain, slight |
| | | Winds light and variable | | | |

# INNER MONGOLIA AND THE WEST HINGAN REGION

## POLITICAL DIVISIONS OF INNER MONGOLIA

"What is to the south of the Great Desert is called Inner Mongolia." So says the *Hui Tien* mentioned above; and though this work also contains detailed descriptions of the extent and boundaries of each banner, they are not accompanied by intelligible

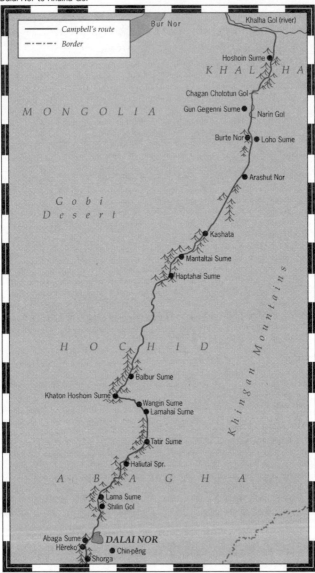

Bur Nor

Khalha Gol (river)

——— Campbell's route
— - — - — Border

Hoshoin Sume

K H A L H A

M O N G O L I A

Chagan Cholotun Gol
Gun Gegenni Sume ● ● Narin Gol

Burte Nor ● ● Loho Sume

● Arashut Nor

G o b i
D e s e r t

● Kashata

● Mantaltai Sume
● Haptahai Sume

H O C H I D

K h i n g a n   M o u n t a i n s

● Balbur Sume

Khaton Hoshoin Sume ●
● Wangin Sume
● Lamahai Sume

● Tatir Sume

● Haliutai Spr.

A   B   A   G   H   A

● Lama Sume
● Shilin Gol

Abaga Sume ●
Hêreko ●        ● Chin-pêng
DALAI NOR
● Shorga

maps, and convey no very definite information. A large portion of the territory therein allotted to Mongol tribes now forms part of Outer Chihli, and the boundaries of most of the banners in the South Hingan region have been altered by Chinese immigration, but the political division of the Inner Mongols into 24 tribes and 49 banners appears to have remained undisturbed by the territorial alterations. The tribes and banners are grouped under six *mêng* or confederations, as set out in the table overleaf.

Each banner is ruled by a hereditary Jassak (Chief), who is well acquainted with the extent of his jurisdiction, and all encroachments on the pastures of other banners are punishable by fine or confiscation of the cattle. There is a hereditary nobility, graded in ranks from *Ch'in-wang* (Prince of the first order) to simple *Taichi* (noble), and these ranks have been conferred for merit or for relationship to the family of Jinghis. The descent and honours of every noble are registered in the Li Fan Yüan, at Peking, and the bearers of hereditary titles indicate their successors, who must be confirmed in the succession by decrees of the Chinese Emperor. On succeeding to a title, a Jassak is summoned to Peking for audience. All the nobility of the Inner Mongol tribes pay visits to the Chinese Court at new year by roster, a cycle of three years completing the roster; and those who do not go to Court are required to attend at the local Jassak's residence on new year's day in full Court dress, and perform the proper obeisances in the direction of Peking. A Jassak presents a sheep and a bottle of milk

| Name of confederation | Name of tribe | Number of banners |
| --- | --- | --- |
| Cherim | Turbet | 1 |
| | Gorlos | 2 |
| | Jelaid | 1 |
| | Khorchin | 6 |
| Chosot | Tumed | 2 |
| | Kharachin | 3 |
| Chao-uda | Aokhan | 1 |
| | Naiman | 1 |
| | Barin | 2 |
| | Jarud | 2 |
| | Aru Khorchin | 1 |
| | Ongniod | 2 |
| | Geshikten | 1 |
| | Khalha | 1 |
| Siling Gol | Uchimuchin | 2 |
| | Khochid | 2 |
| | Sunid | 2 |
| | Abagha | 2 |
| | Abaghanar | 2 |
| Ulan Chap | Durben Keuked | 1 |
| | Mow Mingan | 1 |
| | Urad | 3 |
| | Khalha | 1 |
| Ikhe Chao | Ordos | 7 |

spirit to the Emperor on these occasions, and a Taichi gives a "scalded sheep". Such as visit Peking are banqueted and receive presents of silk, and they attend in the suite of the Chinese Emperor when he goes forth to offer the seasonal sacrifices. At the foundation of the Manchu dynasty, salaries payable by the

Government of China were fixed for Mongol princes and nobles of all ranks, from 2,000 ounces of silver and 25 bales of silk to a *Ch'in-wang*, to 42½ ounces of silver to a noble of the lowest grade; but I am informed that for a period beyond human memory these remunerations have existed only on paper.

The Inner Mongol Jassaks are controlled by the Li Fan Yüan, and occasionally a glimpse of the method of control is to be caught in the pages of the *Peking Gazette*. The following is a translation from the *Gazette* of the 10th March, 1879:

> Prince Darkhan, a Jassak of the Khorchins, was accused of levying fines of so many head of cattle from the Mongols under his jurisdiction, and of wounding some men during a hunting expedition. These accusations were not substantiated, but it was found that he had borrowed money from his subordinates, and this being a most improper proceeding on the part of an official in his position, he was committed by Imperial Decree to the Li Fan Yüan for the determination of a penalty, a step which will be regarded with satisfaction by the Mongol tribes.

These were not the only charges brought against this Jassak; others of arbitrary and tyrannous government were the real causes of attack. We are not told what penalty was eventually inflicted.

## PREVIOUS TRAVELLERS IN EAST MONGOLIA

Kalgan and Dolon-nor, and the roads connecting those two places, are the farthest limits of the vacationist from the China coast. Travel beyond into the arid steppes and uplands north and west involves a sacrifice of time which requires more compensatory attractions than are to be found in this region. There is little or no charm for the tourist; no scenery to speak of, no sport, the nomadic life is simple and not beautiful at close quarters, and the few objects of interest are archaeological relics, unattractive in form and not easily accessible. For two centuries before the era of Treaty relations with China, a sparse succession of Russian missions—ecclesiastical, commercial, and diplomatic—crossed the Gobi by one or other of the caravan routes from Kiakhta to Kalgan, and during the last 40 years, since the Treaties, there has been a continuous, if slender, trickle of foreign travellers—mostly Russian—over the same routes; but they are the only tracks which can be considered beaten by Europeans. Elsewhere, the principal trade roads have been traversed by a number of Russian explorers and pioneers of commerce, but there is still a good deal of blank space on the map—blank space which hardly contains any secrets of moment.

If you set aside the beaten caravan routes between China and Siberia, and the south-eastern border from Dolon-nor to Kuei-hua-ch'êng, few English names occur in the list of Mongolian travellers, and those few turned their attention to regions west of the Kiakhta–Kalgan line. The most notable English name is Ney Elias, and his route was from Kuei-hua-ch'êng to Sair-usu, Uliasutai, Kobdo, and the Russian frontier at Biisk. There is no record of an English traveller in the large space from the Kiakhta routes on the west to the Hingan Mountains on the east. Besides the Jesuit Father Gerbillon, whose journeys date back two centuries, and Dr Franke, of the German Consular Service, I know of none but Russians who have travelled in this space, and the number is small. The prominent names are Fritsche, Przhvalski, and Pozdnyéev.

My route from Dolon-nor to the south-west angle of Dalai Nor, the largest lake of Inner Mongolia, led me almost due north, through Chagan-hota, Mohor Bulak, Shaborte Sume, Shibĕ Sume, Barta, Shorga, and Hêreko. Hêreko (pronounced by Chinese K'o-li-kao, or K'o-li-kêng) is the most out-lying of the permanent Chinese trading settlements in this quarter. I found there three small firms, who barter salt and flour for hides and wool and cattle, and a Chinese population of 50, living in stockaded houses. They were harassed by roving bands of their countrymen, mostly fugitives from justice, who make a bare living by fishing the Dalai Nor in summer. Some of these vagabonds were deserters from the armies who fought around Peking in 1900.

Salt is obtained from many pools and lakes throughout South-East Mongolia, but there is one great salt lake, Dabasun Nor, a week's journey north-west from Dalai Nor, which is the most productive. I constantly came across well-beaten cart-roads (*yen-lu*, "salt roads") leading to this lake, and interminable trains of rude ox-carts were occasionally sighted crawling to Dolon-nor with loads of crude salt. The wheat and oat flour used in the Mongol trade hereabouts comes from Chin-p'êng, a thriving Chinese town situated in a farming district some 25 or 30 miles south-east of Dalai Nor, which, originally a camp of gold-miners clustered around a Geshikten monastery, has grown up in the last half-century, and must now possess 10,000 or 12,000 inhabitants. The Mongol name for Chin-p'êng (Gold Tent) is Piro Hota.

## DALAI NOR TO BURTE NOR

We camped for a couple of days on the shore of Dalai Nor, just beyond the sandhills of Geshikten, and within sight of a prominent Buddhist *stupa* [shrine], known as the Chagan Soberga (White Pagoda). We were now on the border of the Abagha Hoshun. Three rivulets discharged into the south-west corner of the lake—one close to Hêreko, called the Hêreko Gol, another passed on the way to our camp, and Hore Gol, which came from the White Pagoda to a point 300 yards north of our camp. Dalai Nor is a considerable sheet, 16 miles from north-east to south-west, and about 10 miles from east to west. The water has a soda flavour, but it is greenish, clear, and—in the form of tea—drinkable. There are no boats on the lake, and I was unable to examine and sound it, as I had hoped. The whole of the west shore shelves gradually and, by all accounts, the lake is generally shallow, though the Chinese fishermen (who in these matters are not reliable informants) were positive that it was deep in the centre. The same informants were enthusiastic on the abundance of fish of two or three kinds (I myself saw only one species of carp), but lamented that religious scruples of the Abagha Prince interfered with the prosecution of a lucrative fishery. The Prince, as a fervent Buddhist, objected to the lives of the big fish being taken and, in permitting the Chinese to fish, made it a preliminary condition that all the large ones caught should be returned at once to the lake. I saw some reeds on the south shore, which was hilly, and there were many water-birds—geese, ducks of two or three species, sheldrakes, teal, plover, lapwing, redshanks, snippets, gulls, and terns. I noticed also a fishing eagle, kites (*Milvus melanotis*), buzzards (*Buteo desertorum*) and peregrines, chats (*S. ananthe*), larks (*Melanocorypha mongolica*), pipits, ravens, magpies, starlings, sparrows, swallows, and martins.

## Ruins of Ying-ch'ang Fu

Gerbillon stopped at Dalai Nor in 1689, on his remarkable journey with Father Pereira and the Chinese Ambassadors who were sent to Nertschinsk to conclude the first Treaty with Russia; and he mentioned the ruins of a "pagoda" and a marble monument with Chinese inscription, of which he was unable to take a copy. Przhvalski, who circled Dalai Nor in 1871, did not mention ruins, and I concluded that they had disappeared in the course of the two intervening centuries. I was agreeably surprised to hear from our Mongols that there was a *balgas* close by our camp, and I promptly inspected it. It lies 1½ miles from the south-west angle of the lake, under the *stupa* mentioned above. The outer walls are a rectangle, 900 yards from north to south and 800 yards from east to west, and were originally some 20 feet high and 30 feet broad at the base. They are of sandy loam, and are now a succession of longitudinal mounds which, from a quarter of a mile off, might be mistaken for ordinary low sand dunes, and I can easily understand Przhvalski's omission to notice them. The walls face the points of the compass very nearly.

Within there is no general spread of ruins as in Shangtu, and I formed the opinion at once that the original contents were a few important buildings or a royal residence. In the middle of the northern half there are a series of ruins of a palace or temple. Of one large hall, which was 80 feet square, I counted 48 diabase [dolerite] plinths, 4 feet square, still *in situ* in two rows; and in the rear of it there is a rectangle 55 feet by 45 feet, formed of 15 worked plinths of white marble, much damaged, on which, no doubt, rested the pillars of the most important structure. In front of these ruins, to the south, are two black stone (diabase) lions, and more to the south still are the almost unrecognizable trunks of two massive stone tortoises, near which are lying in the grass two mutilated monuments of white marble, with Chinese inscriptions of the Yüan period. In the north-west angle there are two raised mounds, with plinth stones scattered about, and the remains of what must have been a special raised enclosure of considerable dimensions; inside it there is the solitary tree of this deserted city—an aged elm, peopled by noisy starlings and sparrows. There are traces of three gates in the east, west, and south walls, and inside the west gate remains of walls of inferior buildings can be traced. In the south-east angle I noticed two small stone lions (black volcanic stone), and here and there in the east half of the city there are ruins of smaller edifices. No portion of stone wall remains standing; the place must have been razed and the monuments overthrown and defaced. I saw pieces of the royal blue tiles which I found in Shangtu and in Kurtu-balgas (Hsin-liang-ch'êng).

It was evident that Gerbillon's description did not fit these ruins, and I was under the pleasing impression that I was the first European to notice them, until I reached Irkutsk last November. There I bought M. Pozdnyéev's new work on Mongolia, and from the second volume I learnt that in 1893 he had seen the marble monuments answering to Gerbillon's description, and also the ruins I have mentioned above. M. Pozdnyéev quotes from a well-known Chinese book, *Mêng-ku Yu Mu Chi* (Records of the Mongol Nomads), a passage which clearly refers to this place. In AD 1271, Kublai authorized the building of this city, and it was named Ying-ch'ang Fu. Thither the last of the Mongol Emperors, Toghon Timur, fled before the conquering Mings, and there he died in 1368. These old ruins were then the last retreat of the Mongol Court south of the Gobi. The local Mongols called them "Hota" (town) simply, know nothing of their history, and were not much interested when I told them that the Chinese dynastic name of Kublai occurred on one of the marble monuments.

## From Abagha district to Jun Khochid

We followed the whole length of the west shore of Dalai Nor. For a time our route passed over rolling hills, close by two inferior monasteries, Abagha Sume and Dalai Sume, and then a level plain commenced, dotted with clumps of dust-covered *deris* [feather grass] (*Lasiagrostis splendens*) near the lake, but northward we trod on lovely sward, sprinkled with magenta clover, blue flax, yellow vetches, and tall thistles. The plain rose into gentle heights on the north horizon. Evidently the lake had extended over it at no distant period. There was a small *inselberg* [isolated hill] east of us, in the middle of the plain, much water-weathered, and the edges of the low hills to the north-east were water-worn. On the slopes of these hills I counted a herd of 500 hundred *hnang yang* (*Antilope gutturosa*), the largest seen by me in Mongolia. The east shore of the lake, which was easily visible from many eminences, shimmered in the sunlight—the "saline plains" of Przhvalsky. Not far from the north shore we passed a low earth-mound, scarcely noticeable, running east and west, with small hummocks at regular intervals, marking the sites of towers or bastions. The appearance of this rampart, known locally as the Mo-kherim (Bad Wall), suggested to me a greater antiquity than the walls of Ying-ch'ang Fun, and no doubt it is an ancient Chin or Liao barrier. I saw it continue eastward for 7 or 8 miles, and pass out of sight over the hills. The Mongols did not know where it ended, either eastward or westward, and from their remarks I was inclined to believe that it was the same wall which we passed at Mo-kherim, in Chaharia, and which, further west, again is found crossing the Kalgan–Kiakhta caravan routes.

Three days' travel north-north-east took us out of the Abagha district into Jun Khochid (East Banner of the Khochids). The Shilin Gol, a clear stream, with a bed 20 yards wide where we passed it, waters the country immediately to the north of the Dalai basin. Most of the river bed was dry, and the water trickled through sandy reaches, but here and there it gathered into a rapid current over a foot deep. It flows west-ward into a lake, the Mongols said. Near Lama Sume there is a nameless *balgas*, a quarter of a mile square. I observed no trace of stone or brick buildings, and the line of low mounds marking the walls is overgrown with *deris*. In the Lama Sume valley I noticed wild rhubarb for the first time, and a little further north I found a band of Chinese from Chin-p'êng collecting liquorice, which is a common plant on the lower hills. All the Abagha population was clustered around Dalai Nor and in the Shilin Gol valley. I counted 50 or 60 tents about the north shore of the lake, and saw at least 30 in 3 miles of the Shilin Gol, the river pastures being particularly green and abundant; elsewhere we rarely saw a traveller, much less a tent.

Want of water in the south part of Jun Khochid led us to take a more easterly curve through Haliutai, a lone spring bubbling from the rocks in a narrow gulch, to the upper valleys of the Chirin Gol. This is a rivulet of excellent water, formed by two streams which flow from the Hingan Mountains in a north-westerly sweep through the greater part of Jun Khochid. We followed it for two days, past four temples—Tatir Sume, Lamahai Sume, Wangin Sume (Prince's Temple), and Khaton Sume (Lady's Temple). The volume of water decreased—at Khaton Sume, it was the tiniest of brooks—and, according to the Mongols, the Chirin Gol disappears in the sands to the north-west of our route.

## The summer camp of Prince of Jun Khochid

Near Wangin Sume we halted for a night, at the summer encampment of the Prince of Jun Khochid. It was typical, and a description may be of interest. The encampment faced the south-east, the usual orientation of Mongol tents (I found by experience that it was much the best for all weathers). In front there was planted a 20-foot pole, coloured red, with a turned top, gilt; a few paces in the rear of this were two similar poles to right and left, bearing a line of pink and white prayer-pennants, and 15 yards behind was pitched the first tent. It was of the finest new dull white felt, the circular top covering was embroidered and stitched, and it was surmounted by a gilt knob of turned wood, only seen on the abodes of chiefs of banners. The old Prince had died a few months before, and the son, an intelligent-looking youth of 18, kept this chief tent closed during the period of mourning and pending his investiture by the Court of Peking; in any case, it would be used only on occasions of much ceremony. Close behind it there were two tents in line, one large and new-looking, and these were also untenanted in consequence of mourning. Further in the rear in one row were five tents, in which the young Prince and his family were living, and behind these again were three tents for servitors and dependants. Ponies were tethered and picketed on the left front, and there was a constant passage of men and women, mounted and on foot, from the living-tents to the large droves and herds which were cropping the short grass of the steppe, and to the Lama-hai and Prince's temples.

I called on the young Prince (I was the first foreigner he had seen), and was ushered by him into one of the five tents evidently set apart for visits. It was carpeted with felts, which were hemmed and stitched, and over them were laid square wool rugs, on which we sat. With the exception of four, all the Princes and Jassaks of the 49 banners of the Inner Mongols are descendants of Jinghis or his brothers, and according to the *Hui Tien*, this young Khochid Prince is of the family of Torobolod, or Turubolod, who was sixteenth in descent from Jinghis himself.

## Uchimuchin

A guide sent to us by the Khochid Prince led us from Khaton Sume and the Chirin Gol on a straight course to the Khalha River and Khailar. To Balbur Nor we passed over a belt of sand hillocks similar to those of Geshikten, by swampy pools edged with sedges and rushes and swarming with mosquitoes, and through moist troughs studded with small elms and dwarf willows. Balbur Sume, a large temple of 700 lamas and a *gegen* (minor lamaistic incarnation), lies north-east of the lake, and here I noticed three well-worn caravan tracks, leading from Manchuria to the middle course of the Kerulon. On the morning of the 15th July we entered the territory of Ikhe Uchimuchin (Great Uchimuchin), under the leadership of a delightful old noble (*Taichi*); on the 21st July we reached Baga (Little) Uchimuchin; and on the 23rd July, within three days' march of the Khalha Gol, the boundary line of Inner Mongolia was crossed, and we entered Khalha territory.

Uchimuchin resembles the Chahar country, but the plains dividing the low rounded hills are sandy, arid, or nitrous, in parts almost desert. For two or three days the want of pasture gave me some anxiety. The season was exceptionally dry, I was told, and the Mongols in some places were oppressed by the severity of the drought, which had killed large numbers of sheep. Uchimuchin is famous for ambling ponies, and certainly the breed was noticeably larger and finer than in Khochid, Abagha, Geshikten, and the Chahar country, but it is much exploited for the horse-markets of Manchuria (Ku-lieh'rh appeared to be the principal of these), and prices of good-looking animals were absurdly high. In Uchimuchin primitive carts of wood, which came all the way from Khalha River, were in general use. A slender ring of cast-iron bushing inserted in the nave of the axle to work on is the only bit of metal used in the construction of these vehicles. Every *ail*, every tent had its carts; special water-carts, travelling carts, roofed in with felt, and open carts for collecting *argol* [dried dung used for fuel] and general purposes. Oxen were the usual draught animals, and the drivers in short excursions were invariably women.

Near Burte Nor, which is in Baga Uchimuchin, but close to the Khalha border, we joined the main caravan road between Khailar and Dolon-nor. The traffic was inconsiderable, but striking after the loneliness of the previous three weeks: two small Mongol trains of ox-carts, bearing timber to Ikhe Uchimuchin from the Khalha Gol, and a large caravan (50 carts) belonging to Chinese traders of Khailar, who were transporting the season's collection of hides, sheepskins, and poles to Dolon-nor. Khailar being a station on the Manchurian line, I asked these men why they did not use the railway; they complained of the cost of carriage, which would swamp all their profits, but I gathered that their real objection was the difficulty of changing long-established habits of business.

Since my return to England I have seen a lately published book, in which it is alleged that a railway is

## Temperature in Hingan region from Dolon-nor to Lake Bur

| Name of place | Date (1902) | Temperature (degrees F) | | | Remarks |
|---|---|---|---|---|---|
| | | 7 am | 2 pm | 9 pm | |
| Chagan-hota | June 28 | — | 66.5 | 58.5 | |
| | 29 | 59.8 | — | 58.8 | Heavy thunder-storms, with hail |
| *En route* | 30 | 60.6 | 73.2 | — | |
| Mohor-bulak | 30 | — | — | 55 | |
| | July 1 | 61.5 | — | — | Rain, medium showers |
| Shaborte | 1 | — | 75 | — | |
| Camp | 1 | — | — | 60.3 | |
| *En route* | 2 | 64.6 | 76.2 | 57 | |
| Holeba | 3 | — | 85.1 | — | |
| *En route* | 3 | — | — | 63.6 | |
| | 4 | 67.4 | — | — | |
| Dalai Nor | 4 | — | 85.4 | 63.6 | Rain, light showers |
| | 5 | 65.8 | 75.3 | — | |
| | 6 | 66.3 | 75.8 | 72 | |
| *En route* | 7 | 75 | 89.9 | 71 | |
| | 8 | 61.6 | 75.3 | 58.6 | |
| | 9 | 59.5 | 75.4 | — | |
| Haliutai Spring | 8 | — | — | 57 | |
| *En route* | 10 | 67.5 | 84.4 | — | |
| Tatir Sume | 10 | — | — | 69.8 | |
| *En route* | 11 | 75.5 | 82.2 | — | |
| Lamahai Sume | 11 | — | — | 71 | |
| | 12 | 65.7 | — | — | |
| Khaton Sume | 12 | — | 73.4 | 60.4 | |
| | 13 | 57 | — | 56.2 | |
| *En route* | 14 | 60.1 | 75 | — | |
| Balbur Sume | 14 | — | — | 59.5 | |
| *En route* | 15 | 63.2 | 78.5 | 61.2 | |
| | 16 | 68.2 | 91.6 | 73.8 | |
| | 17 | 72.4 | 80.2 | 68 | |
| | 18 | 68.2 | — | — | |

| Name of place | Date (1902) | Temperature (degrees F) | | | Remarks |
|---|---|---|---|---|---|
| | | 7 am | 2 pm | 9 pm | |
| Mantal-tai Sume | July 18 | — | 89.6 | 67.5 | |
| | 19 | 71 | — | — | |
| Kashata | 19 | — | — | 71.8 | |
| | 20 | 69 | 91.5 | 70.7 | |
| *En route* | 21 | 62.4 | 72.8 | 66.8 | |
| | 22 | 68.7 | 83.6 | 63 | |
| | 23 | 66.5 | — | — | |
| Burte Nor | 23 | — | 85.9 | — | |
| *En route* | 23 | — | — | 71.2 | |
| | 24 | 60.5 | 71.6 | — | |
| Chagan Cholotun Gol | 24 | — | — | 65 | |
| *En route* | 25 | 63.1 | 70.5 | — | |
| Hoshoin Sume | 25 | — | — | 58.8 | |
| *En route* | 26 | 64.5 | — | — | |
| Khalha Gol | 26 | — | 87.4 | 71.3 | |
| | 27 | 65.5 | 70.8 | 67.5 | |
| | 28 | 68.3 | 73.8 | 64.3 | |
| | 29 | 63.2 | — | — | |
| Ikhe Borhan Sume | 29 | — | 76.7 | 64.3 | |
| *En route* | 30 | 60.2 | 69.8 | — | |
| Khalha Gol | 30 | — | — | 60.6 | |
| | 31 | 58.5 | — | — | |
| Khalha Hoshoin Sume | 31 | — | — | 59.5 | |
| Bur Nor | 31 | — | — | 59.5 | |
| | August 1 | 62.4 | 75 | 61.5 | |

being pushed surreptitiously from the neighbourhood of Khailar southward to Kalgan, and this
statement has been given some publicity in the press.
In July 1902 I travelled over a portion of the trace
marked in this book, and saw no signs of the railway.
The Manchurian line was constantly spoken of, but
no Mongol or Chinese (and I met three or four

traders who had come directly from Khailar across the route of the alleged railway) ever said a word of a new branch coming southward.

I add a series of daily minimum temperatures which are trustworthy. As I marched regularly during the period of greatest heat, I was not able to obtain reliable maximum temperatures.

| Date (1902) | Minimum temperature | Date (1902) | Minimum temperature |
|---|---|---|---|
| | Degrees F | | Degrees F |
| June 25 | 41.6 | July 14 | 48 |
| 27 | 43.7 | 16 | 59.5 |
| 28 | 38.8 | 17 | 55.4 |
| July 1 | 43.8 | 18 | 56.4 |
| 2 | 48.5 | 21 | 51 |
| 3 | 45.3 | 22 | 47.7 |
| 4 | 47.7 | 23 | 57.3 |
| 5 | 45.2 | 24 | 55 |
| 6 | 56 | 25 | 47.5 |
| 7 | 57.2 | 26 | 57.8 |
| 8 | 35.8 | 27 | 52.7 |
| 9 | 40.5 | 28 | 51.8 |
| 10 | 63.2 | 29 | 49.8 |
| 11 | 47.3 | 30 | 53.8 |
| 12 | 53 | 31 | 55.6 |
| 13 | 42.4 | August 1 | 50.5 |

# THE KHALHA KHANATES

The Khalha Khanates, into the most eastern of which we have now penetrated, extend from the Khalha River westward for more than 1,000 miles to beyond Uliasutai. On the north they march with the Siberian frontier; on the south they are stopped by the Gobi; Kalmuck peoples are their neighbours on the west; and on the east they are hemmed in by the Barukh (Barhu or Barhut) banners and Uchimuchin. And let me state here that though the exact boundaries of

Khalha Gol to Para-hota

these tribal divisions are not accurately indicated on any European map, they are none the less well-known to the Mongols, and carefully observed. Even in the Gobi, which, in East Mongolia at any rate, is not the stony waste it is generally conceived to be, the political limits of the Inner and Outer Mongols follow a recognized boundary which appears to date back to Ming times.

There are four Khanates of the Khalhas. Beginning from the east these are:

Tsetsen Khanate, comprising 23 banners.
Tushetu Khanate, comprising 20 banners.
Jassaktu Khanate, comprising 18 banners.
Sainnoin Khanate, comprising 22 banners.

In addition to the 83 banners of true Khalhas, there are three Kalmuck banners which are included in Khalha territory, making 86 in all. Urga, which I shall describe later on, is the administrative capital of the East Khalhas (Tsetsen and Tushetu Khanates); the two western Khanates are ruled by the Manchu Chiang-chün (Military Governor) of Uliasutai.

Each banner, as in Inner Mongolia, is under a *Jassak* [chief], whose titular rank may vary from simple Taichi to Ch'in-wang. The Jassaks and leading nobles are mostly descendants of Jinghis. I quote a translation from the *Peking Gazette* of the 30th June, 1878, which describes characteristically the form of investiture of a Jassak:

Memorial by Ngo-lo-ho-pu, Military Governor at Uliasutai, and the two Assistant Governors, conveying

the thanks of Prince To-erh-ki-p'a-la-ma, *Jassak* (or
Chief) of the Jassakt'u tribe, one of the four great
divisions of the Khalha nation, for permission to
succeed to the title. He had received a
communication from the Prince to the effect that he
was in receipt of instructions from the Li Fan Yüan,
stating that they had been informed by the Mêng
Chang (or Captain-General) of the Jassakt'u tribe,
that it was proposed to give the vacant title of *To-lo
Chün Wang* (or Prince of the Second Order over the
Jassakt'u tribe) to the Duke T'o-erh-ki-p'a-la-ma, the
son of the late Prince, who had recommended him
for the succession. As, however, T'o-erh-ki-p'a-la-ma,
who was 21 years of age, had not yet had the small-
pox, he could not go to Peking. The Captain-General
requested that this fact might be reported to His
Majesty. The name of Duke T'o-erh-ki-p'a-la-ma, son
of the late Ch'e-lin-jui-to-pu, by whom he was
recommended for the succession, was also appended
to this representation. The Li Fan Yüan having
reported the matter to His Majesty, the Imperial
sanction was obtained to the succession, and the Li
Fan Yüan had to instruct him, the Prince, to that
effect. As he read this communication while kneeling
reverently upon the ground, the Prince was filled
with the deepest gratitude. He immediately took over
his seals of office and entered upon his duties. While
humbly acknowledging himself to be a Mongol slave
of inferior ability, perfectly unable to repay in the
slightest degree the Imperial favours of which his
family have been the recipients for generations past,

he declares his intention of performing his duties to the best of his feeble powers. In accordance with precedent, he turned himself towards the Palace and beat his head upon the ground at Uliasutai on the 5th of the 4th moon, in grateful acknowledgement of the Imperial bounty, and he now begged the memorialist [recorder] to inform His Majesty of the fact, which, as in duty bound, memorialist hereby does.

## KHALHA RIVER TO ULAN NOR

On Saturday, the 26th July, we pitched camp on the Khalha River, near a prominent bluff of limestone named Krei Ul, which marks the boundary between two banners of the Tsetsen Khanate. Here the river emerges from the hills and splits into two channels and some back-water creeks. The bed is gravel and sand, and the water soft and pure and running in places to 4 or 5 feet in depth. At the ford in front of our camp it was deep enough (2 feet) to cover the axles of the ox-carts, and from the way the cattle and camels crossed it at will to pasture on either bank, I gathered that it was not difficult to find a fording-place. From the top of Krei Ul I saw that the river wound north-westward between sandhills and bluffs, its course marked by a narrow *bourgas* (thicket) of willow, hawthorn, elm, currant, etc.; that the river basin, as distinct from the unwatered grey-green uplands, averaged less than 3 miles wide; that this basin was moist emerald meadow, interspersed with marshes and pools; and that it was evidently subject to inundation during strong summer freshets [floods]. It was the richest and most populous part of Mongolia which I had seen up to then. I counted 200 tents in a day's march, nearly all on the north side of the river; the flocks and herds were continuous, and the tents were nearly all new and good. Eastward, in the direction where the celebrated Soyelki Shan is marked on the Chinese maps (I know of no European who has visited this mountain), I noticed hills of no considerable height—none more than 800 or 1,000 feet above the river-level.

## Monastery of the Large Buddha

We followed the south bank of the Khalha River for four days to a crossing-place near the embouchure [river mouth] into Lake Bur. The most remarkable place in this section of the river is Ikhe Borhan Sume (Monastery of the Large Buddha), which was being repaired by Chinese masons and carpenters imported for the purpose from Dolon-nor. The enterprise of these men can be judged from the fact that they made the journey in a month on foot, practically working their way, for they started with light purses. They told me that their remuneration was equivalent to 7 or 8 ounces of silver (1*l.*) a month. Everywhere in East Mongolia the temples and monasteries are repaired by itinerant Chinese workmen, the Mongols themselves being unable to do such work and unwilling to learn. Ikhe Borhan Sume is built on the incline of low hills bordering the river, and contains a recumbent image of Kuan-yin (Avalokiteswara), which lies in an open sloping courtyard and is conspicuous for miles. The figure is a rude fabrication of stone and mortar, whitened with lime and ornamented with coloured washes, 40 feet long and 30 feet broad, and more antique than most of the East Mongol shrines. Outside the main buildings a rough low wall of piled stones protected a curious border of Tibetan letters—each letter was 15 feet square, and neatly formed of stones hammered into the hillside—which ran along the edges and top of the temple enclosure. I distinguished this Tibetan prayer with my Zeiss glasses [binoculars] from a distance of 2 miles. Close by the river there is a very large and sacred *obo* and the remains of an ancient shrine, which had suffered from inundation.

Here I met an itinerant Russian trader, with a Buriat interpreter, who was bartering Russian cloths, purple and red cottons, copper kettles, enamel ware, tinned ladles, matches, etc. for cattle, sheep, and wool. It was a new venture, and he was not entirely satisfied with the success of it. From him I received confirmation of a report which had reached me a few days previously, that cholera was rife in Khailar.

**Bur Nor**

At our point of crossing near the Bur Nor, the Khalha River was split into two channels; the broader was 120 yards across, but shallow. Neither it nor the narrow channel, which was only 20 yards broad, ran deeper than 2½ to 3 feet. West of the crossing a thick growth of dwarf willow hid the view. The country was perfectly flat, and very slightly raised above the level of the lake. We camped at Khalha Hoshoin Sume on the Ursun Gol, which carries the overflow from Bur Nor to Kulun Nor. So slight was this on the 1st August, that I could scarcely discern the trend of the current. I followed the Ursun to the lake, which, though only 3 miles in a direct line south from the monastery, was quite invisible from it. At Khalha Hoshoin Sume this river was 100 yards wide and easily fordable. It winds in gentle curves, spreading into a morass in one or two places, and the stream broadens as one nears the Bur Nor. Where it leaves the lake there are two tiny islets, and it was sufficiently shallow to allow a drove of ponies to take refuge in it from the flies.

A little east of south and half-a-dozen miles off, a thicket of dwarf willow marked the place where the Khalha Gol disemboges [disgorges]. Across the lake to the west, an imposing yellow mass quivering in the belt of heated air, was Asar Sume, a Barukh monastery. From west to south the Bur Nor extended "*à perte de vue*" ["as far as the eye can see"], and the slight breeze there was had lashed it into a thundering sea. There is not a boat on the lake, and no one has ever ventured to cross it. The Mongols, as usual, said that it was unfathomable. The shores were covered with wild-fowl—geese, ducks, plovers, gulls, terns, lapwing, cormorants, waders of many species—and a few conspicuous ospreys hovered over the Ursun, which was alive with fish. Two Mongols were spearing successfully—the only Mongol fishermen I have seen—and I bought some turbot and an 8-lb carp from them.

At Khalha Hoshoin Sume we passed across the Ursun Gol into Barukh territory. The Barukhs occupy the region north of the Khalha River and Bur Nor, are organized into eight banners under much the same conditions as the Chahars, and are controlled by a Manchu official usually stationed at Khailar, which is known throughout East Mongolia as Amban Hota (Governor Town). The Barukh banners were summoned to arms in 1900 to oppose the Russian occupation, and from the temporary sadness which overtook most Barukhs when the subject was broached, I gathered that the experience was unpleasant. I heard later that the Khailar Amban had provoked hostilities by attacks on inoffensive Russian traders, in which the Barukhs displayed some audacity, but that the first skirmish with Russian troops—a short affair in which 200 or 300 Mongols lost their lives—sent the Barukhs to their tents and tranquillized North-East Mongolia completely. I have small doubt that the Chahar banners could be pacified just as easily.

It was my intention to follow the Ursun Gol to Kulun Nor, and to make an excursion to Khailar before turning westward towards Urga, but at Ulan Nor I heard that the cholera was more virulent than ever, that it had reached Ganjur Sume, a trading centre only 30 miles off, and that cases had occurred on the Ursun; and we saw Mongols trekking night and day westward in consequence. This form of cholera does not appear to be dangerous to Europeans who are careful of their diet, but I felt that it was hopeless to expect the necessary amount of caution from my followers, and forthwith decided to make for the Kerulon. Ulan Nor (Red Lake) is the "Oulan Poulac" (Red Spring) of Gerbillon. It is a long, narrow lagoon running westward from the Ursun, and renowned for its pastures. Here, in 1698, Gerbillon spent a week in the suite of the High Commissioners who were sent by the Emperor Kang-hsi to hold the first council of the Khalha Princes, and Gerbillon's journal remained for 200 years the solitary description in European literature of the Bur-Dalai (Coupled Oceans), as this lake-region is called by the local Mongols.

## ULAN NOR TO URGA

On our way north-west to the Kerulon I ascended a prominent hill named Bogdo Ul (God's Mount), and obtained a remarkable view of the stretch of country between the lakes. Bogdo Ul rises only 1,000 feet above the level of the Ursun Gol, but it towers over all the neighbouring heights, and was first noticed by me from an eminence south of the Khalha River, 50 miles away. It is a limestone rock, surmounted by a collection of *obo*, which are much visited by pilgrims. A few gnarled elms grew in the folds and gave shelter to some buntings and warblers, and I saw dwarfed specimens of wild rhubarb amongst the scanty herbage. To the east and south the view was unbounded, and was lost in a dim grey rift, which I took to be the Bur Nor; on the west and north it was limited by hills, those on the north being high and bold. With my glasses I distinguished the brown marshland of the south shore of Kulun Nor and the waters of the lake beyond it. I failed to observe a trace of the Kerulon, and I understood the reason when I reached the bank of this famous river next day.

## The Kerulon River

My acquaintance with the Kerulon (pronounced Khérelon by the Khalhas) began on the 5th August, at a point less than two days' march from its entrance into Kulun Nor, and 5 or 6 miles south-west of the Altan Emûl (Golden Saddle), a pair of brown hills famous in Mongol legend, between which the river flows. With the exception of one large bend which we cut across, we kept along the river westward for 300 miles, to the seat of the Tsetsen Khan; passed it further west on the 2nd September; and in the third week of September I followed it once more from the neighbourhood of Jun Khure to one of its sources in the Kentei Mountains.

The Kerulon River is the Jordan of the Mongols. As Gerbillon said two centuries ago, it is an inconsiderable river, but the longest in the vast arid East Mongol upland, and the permanence of the pastures along its banks has always attracted a large share of the nomad population. Many of the Tsetsen princes keep their headquarters on or close to the Kerulon. An irregular belt of green meadow, blotched by occasional brown marsh, follows the course of the stream, and varies from a mere riband to 4 or 5 miles in width; outside the meadows there is the ordinary steppe, often nitrous, or low hills, granite or sandstone, of a more irregular type than in East and South-East Mongolia. Near Altan Emul there were two channels wriggling through the meadows a short distance apart, the largest 18 yards broad and unfordable; the current was dark and troubled, and ran 3 or 4 miles an hour. Chagan Dure Nor, the Doure Nor of D'Anville's map, is a lagoon formed by overflow from the river. Dwarf willows lined the banks at intervals, but there was no trace of forest vegetation on the steppe and hills, which were covered with artemisia, steppe acacia (*Caragana*), wild onion, *Potentilla*, and grasses (*Agropyrum*).

## Sam Beise Urgo

At Mergen Ul (11th August) the Kerulon is confined for a couple of miles in a gorge of sandstone hills, through which the stream, still coloured by dark alluvium [silt], rushed with increased current. The boundary between the Barukh banners and the Tsetsen Khanate was passed a few miles west of Mergen Ul, and on the 13th August we arrived at Sam Beise Urgo, which is marked on Russian maps as "Kerulon". The names of any but the very prominent physical features are always doubtful in Mongolia, but the traveller has special difficulty in dealing with the political sub-divisions of the Tsetsen Khanate. To give an instance: for years I had heard at Peking of a district called by the Chinese "Minchasa", from which excellent specimens of the Mongol pony came to us regularly. I never could discover exactly where it was; my Chinese informants could only say it was "behind" and "very far", and none of the Mongols I came across had ever heard of it. It was only when I was within a day's march of Sam Beise Urgo that I learnt that the district known to the Mongols as Sam Beise was identical with the Chinese Minchasa. The sub-divisions of the mid-Kerulon country are named after the chiefs of the moment, and Minchasa is a Chinese pronunciation of Min Jassak (Chief Min), the grandfather of the present prince (named Sanselei Dordji), who is styled shortly Sam Beise (Prince Sam or San). Min Jassak ruled for a long period, and the Chinese traders, who are accustomed to attach permanent names to places, continue to use the designation by which this part of the Kerulon Valley first became known to them.

Sam Beise Urgo (seat of Prince San) is the principal trading-place on the Kerulon; caravan routes from Urga, Khailar, and the Siberian and Chinese frontiers pass through it. There are two large monasteries on the north bank of the river, and in the neighbourhood live the representatives of 40 Chinese firms of Peking, Kalgan, and Dolon-nor, who patiently barter silks and miscellaneous luxuries for cattle, ponies, hides, and wool. The oldest of these firms had commenced business on this spot 70 years previously. During the Boxer convulsion of 1900 they were all plundered and driven away at the instigation of some enterprising Russians, and at the time of my visit the prince and his subjects were performing, under pressure from Peking and Urga, the disagreeable duty of indemnifying the sufferers, whose claims, of course, exceeded the most sanguine estimates. Curiously enough I had met, close to Khara-balgas, in Chaharia, a band of the chief offenders in this robbery, who were under escort to Peking for trial and punishment: it was a striking illustration of what the Chinese Government can do in the administration of justice when they are in earnest. These men had ridden 1,000 miles, and would ride 200 miles more on their own ponies to expiate an offence of no special enormity, and the duty of escorting them was entrusted to a few of their own friends and neighbours.

The Sambeise Administrator paid me a formal call, and I returned it at his yamên, a felt tent of no exceptional size, where all the business of the banner was transacted and justice administered. A brazier filled with glowing argol [fuel made from dung] occupied the centre, and the Administrator himself sat on a mat behind it and opposite the door. Around were mats on which various officers were sitting, and on the left two scribes were copying laboriously a scored draft in Mongol writing. Each used a small wooden board, which they held with one hand as they wrote with the other on flimsy Chinese paper with a Chinese pencil. They were not skilled pens-men. I was struck by the illiteracy of all these men: when my passport, an ordinary document, was sub-mitted for examination, they seemed to read the easiest passages with the greatest difficulty.

The normal population of the tent was at least ten persons—messengers, clerks, and officers—and there was a constant babble of conversation. The Chief looked harassed, and made no secret of the rea-son: five new Chinese claimants had come to demand satisfaction. Business was not allowed to interfere with his devotions, for while he was attending to me and issuing orders to messengers and assistants, he turned a prayer cylinder of sheet copper which stood on a low table beside him.

At Sam Beise Urgo the Kerulon was 30 to 40 yards wide and easily fordable; the bed was sandy and the water fairly clear. I noticed a "dug-out" at one of the fords, and was told that it was usually required during summer freshets [floods]. We crossed the river at Sam Beise, and followed the caravan route along the north bank through the territory of several ban-ners to the seat of the Tsetsen Khan, who is *primus inter pares* [first among equals] of the East Khalha princes.

**Para-hota**

The ruins of Para-hota (Tiger Town) were reached on the 20th August. They were seen by Gerbillon in 1698, and his short description might stand for the

Para-hota to Urga

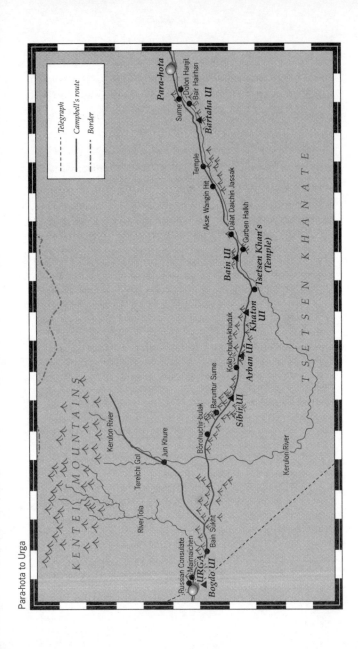

present day. There are "grands pans de muraille de terre", but he exaggerated the extent. I paced two sides, and found the enclosure a rectangle of 1,600 yards by 1,400 yards. The earth-walls are now long, grass-grown mounds, 4 to 5 feet high in the centre, and 30 feet broad, and outside them there are traces of a ditch. Three hundred yards from the centre of the west wall and outside the enclosure there is one of the "pyramids" of Gerbillon. It is a *dagoba* [dome-shaped structure] of brick, and it seems a marvel that a structure of the kind, which was "half-ruined" in 1698, should be erect in 1902. It is crumbling, but still stands, and its 40 feet of height make it a prominent landmark.

Inside the city, and some 200 yards from the centre of the south wall, there is the other of Gerbillon's pyramids in much the same condition. It is also a *dagoba* or *chorten* of brick, 30 feet high. Near it I observed a large mound, 30 yards square and 4 feet high, of building debris—rubble stones, broken bricks, and fragments of marble, but no blue tiles or potsherds. Besides this I saw a few heaps of stones, which might have been the sites of buildings; but the rest of the enclosure was a flat expanse of steppe, which could not have been much built over at any time. Para-hota (Klaproth rendered it Bars-hotun, from a transliteration of Chinese ideographs) is a relic of the Yüan dynasty, and is said to have been founded by Toghon Timur in the middle of the fourteenth century.

## Other temples and monasteries along the Kerulon

The Khalha chieftains, whose seats I had an opportunity of examining—Sam Beise, Batur Jassak, Akhse Wang (these two chiefs had died recently), Dalai Datchin Jassak, Tsetsen Jassak—were housed in the national dwellings, Mongol *gher* (circular felt tents); but the residence of the Tsetsen Khan is a permanent brick-and-tile structure of the Chinese type, and if it were not for a private chapel built into the south-west angle, distinguished by red walls and a gilt ornament on the roof, I should not have hesitated to class it as a second-rate Chinese yamên. All these chiefs live in the neighbourhood of their territorial monasteries, which are the only fixed habitations here as elsewhere in East and North Mongolia. They are, as a rule, of brick; along the Khalha and Kerulon I saw a few which were almost wholly of timber. In most there are pavilions and porticoes differing slightly from those of Chinese Buddhistic temples, but the design of the principal chapel is often pure Tibetan.

On the 29th August we broke camp from the Tsetsen Khan's headquarters, left the Kerulon—which continues south-westward for another 100 miles before turning sharply to the north—and steered a direct course for Urga. The Taragilch Gol, the first perennial affluent of the Kerulon met with, was passed between two notable hills called "The Lord" and "The Lady" (Noyon Ul and Khaton Ul); and thenceforward, with a few short intervals of plain, we were constantly making fairly sharp ascents or descents until the Kerulon Valley was struck again. The higher hills were granite, and they appeared to burst through strata of shale and slate; the castings from the many marmot [type of rodent] burrows were invariably a sharp gravel of shale or slate. The noteworthy *cols* [passes] were the Hannûngin Daban (3,700 feet) and the Joldûngin Daban (4,000 feet), both of which taxed the temper and strength of the cart-camel.

From the Joldûngin Daban we descended into the narrow valley of the Chinkir Gol, another affluent of the Kerulon, and west of it, on Sibir Ul, we saw for the first time in these parts a slender fringe of pine forest. At the Tsetsen Khan's seat the Kerulon was more than 100 yards wide, but fordable everywhere; the bed was sand and gravel, and the water still clouded with sediment. When we passed it on the 2nd September it was split into two swift, clear streams, a mile apart, both of which were formidable obstacles to carts. On the 4th September we crossed the water-parting into the valley of the Tola, and next day reached Urga and the bounteous hospitality of my friend, Mr von Grot, and other members of the Russian colony.

# *URGA*

The first observation of the traveller who approaches from the south is that Urga enjoys a surprising supply of perennial water. The valley runs east and west, and from the north-east hills the Tola issues, pellucid and pure, splits its channel here and there, bends down towards the Bogdo Ul, waters the whole 20 miles of the valley's length, and curves out of sight in the south-west, near the willows of Sangin. East of Mai-mai-chên (Chinese Urga) one crosses four separate

Journeys from Urga

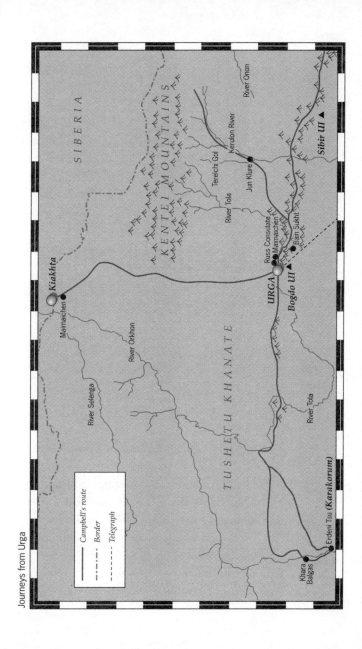

water-courses within hailing distance of each other—
the two largest by substantial wooden bridges
constructed at the cost of the Russian Consulate-
General; and between Mai-mai-chên and Gandan,
the west end of Mongol Urga, there are a few brooks
trickling into the Tola, which in summer are useful
and convenient auxiliaries. A mile or so south of the
Tola the long, low mass of the Bogdo Ul closes the
view completely. Northward from it, to the Tola and
beyond, there is an irregular space of fairly level but
stony ground, which is 6 or 7 miles broad at its
widest; along the north fringe of this, and on the ter-
races and spurs footing the inconsiderable hills which
hem the valley on the north, are scattered the curious
collection of settlements and temples comprehended
in the name Urga.

## HISTORY OF URGA

Urga, the Russian pronunciation of the Mongol word
*örgo* (residence), is scarcely known to Mongols. The
full native name is Bogdo Lamain Khure (The God-
lama's Encampment); shorter names are Da Khure
or Ikhe Khure (Great Encampment), Bogdo Khure,
or simply Khare. The Chinese call the place K'u-lun
or K'u-lien, or Ta (Great) K'u lien—K'u-lun or K'u-
lien being an attempt to pronounce the Mongol word
*Khure*. Urga is the administrative centre of the East
Khalha Khanates, and the Rome of all Mongols. Its
history appears to begin in the middle of the seventeenth century with the institution of the "Bogdo" as

the Pontiff of the Lamaistic Church in North Mongolia. This Mongol Pope seems to rank as the third in importance of the great avatars, or "living gods", of Lamaism, coming after the Dalai Lama of Lhassa and the Pantshen Lama of Tashilunpo, and occupies a political position in the Mongol world analogous to that of the popes of mediaeval Christendom. The ecclesiastical title is *Cheptsun Damba Khutukhtu*, which was originally conferred by the Dalai Lama of Tibet in AD 1650 or 1651 on a son of the Tushetu Khan.

This Prince was the St Paul of Mongol Lamaism, and is known in Mongol history as Undur Gegen. Under his advice the Khalha tribes gravitated to China, rather than to Russia, in 1688, when the attacks of the Kalmucks under Galdan threatened their existence. He is the "Grand Lama Houtouktou" who figures so largely in Gerbillon's description of the assembly of the Khalha Princes held by Kang-hsi at Dolon-nor in 1691. Although the first "incarnation" living in Mongolia, and really the first Bogdo, he is ecclesiastically considered to have had 15 predecessors, who lived in India and Tibet, from the time of Sakyamuni, and the present Bogdo is the eighth in succession from him. His Pontificate lasted for 70 years, and placed the influence of the Lamaistic Papacy completely above that of any territorial prince. He was succeeded by a newly born Mongol Princeling in 1724, but the selection of the second Bogdo was attended by much intrigue, and gave rise to intertribal dissensions in which the Chinese Government foresaw political trouble. The Bogdo's power, too, required clipping. On the death of the second Bogdo, in 1757, it was arranged that the new "incarnation" should come from Tibet, and since then the Urga Popes have all been Tibetans of no special family influence.

At the time of Undur Gegen, it would appear that the Bogdo had only a temporary residence at Urga, and Mongol annals tell us of many places in South-East and North Mongolia where he lived for short or long periods. In 1756 the Tsanit college for the instruction of the Lamaistic priesthood in the Buddhism of Tibet was founded in Gandan; thenceforward the residence of the Bogdo appears to have been fixed, and Urga became the religious centre of North Mongolia. From the very beginning the Chinese Government recognized the influence wielded by the Bogdo over the Khalhas, and so long as they were satisfied—as they were during the period of Undur Gegen—that the influence would be used entirely in their favour, no attempt was made to circumscribe it; but political clouds gathered in the second Bogdo's reign, and a steady dispersal of his influence became the note of the Chinese policy. Under the pretext of the sanctity of his person, measures were taken to restrict his individual power to religious matters only, and in 1754 secular concerns were handed over to a chosen body of *shabinars* (papal serfs).

After the death of the second Bogdo, a Mongol governor was appointed by Imperial Decree to superintend the work of these *shabinars*, and in 1761 a

Manchu Amban [resident official] from Peking was appointed as coadjutor. In 1786 the increasing importance of Urga made it necessary to advance the status of the Ambans, and the administrative control over the Tushetu and Tsetsen Aimaks, which had hitherto rested with the Governor-General (Chiang-chün) of Uliasutai, was transferred to them. Urga now became the political capital of North-East Mongolia, and soon attracted a settled population.

## URGA IN 1902

In 1902 Urga was in three distinct portions. By far the largest is the Mongol town; this comprises Urga proper—Lamaseries [lama monasteries] of the Bogdo with an attendant and now miscellaneous population, and Gandan, where the Tsanit temples and schools are established. A mile-and-a-half to the east, on a low incline, stands the Russian Consulate, and near it are clustered a half-dozen Russian compounds, the nucleus of a Russian settlement. Beyond to the east, and a couple of miles further on, is the Chinese Mai-mai-chên (trade borough). All three portions, as I have mentioned, lie to the north of the Tola, and the total population cannot fall much short of 25,000, of whom one-half are lamas.

The heart of the Mongol town is the Bogdo's palace and the temples for general worship, of which the principal is the Tsokchin. There are in addition 28 other temples, each the special shrine of an ecclesiastical sub-division of the Khalha peoples, but these are

largely composed of felt tents, and are far inferior to
the Tsokchin, Maidari and other chief places of worship. Where these are, open spaces abound, but
elsewhere Mongol Urga is a collection of blocks of
palisaded enclosures containing low squalid huts, and
separated by narrow streets and lanes, in which
wheeled traffic is rare. Prayer wheels of large size,
sheltered by wooden sheds, are numerous in all the
wider spaces, and by a touch of the hand as you pass
along it is possible to say more prayers in five minutes
than the glibbest tongue could repeat in a month.

Away from the temples Urga is a dull, sombre
place, and people acquainted with the inner life have
nothing attractive to report about it. I was chiefly
interested in the market-place, where I spent a few
mornings chaffering [haggling] with the bright
matrons who kept most of the stalls for silver head-
dresses, pipes, snuff-bottles, hats, leather boots, sashes,
Buddhistic pictures, and miscellaneous curios of no
great value. Near the stalls half-a-dozen camels were
awaiting purchasers; flocks of sheep were tightly
folded close by a bevy of eager women selling hats; a
score of ponies for sale were bunched up behind a
tangle of carts, on which Mongol butchers were
rapidly dissecting carcases of mutton; here a Chinese
itinerant blacksmith, there a carpenter or tinker; and
everywhere the good-humoured motley throng of
Mongols from all parts, sprinkled with Russian
Buriats and a few Tibetans. The vicinity of the market-
place is occupied by several shops of Russian traders,
and a small settlement of Chinese merchants.

There was a time when women and traders were forbidden to live in this town (in 1763 a decree of Ch'ien-lung forbade the presence of women in Khure "where the Hutukhtu lives"), and all commerce was carried on in Mai-mai-chên, the Chinese town which is ten *li* to the east. This was at first a stockaded enclosure with six gates, which are still closed at sunset. It was established in the early part of the eighteenth century as a residence for the Chinese trading population. Nowadays there is a cluster of Mongol suburbs outside the palisade, and the settled community numbers 4,000 or 5,000, of whom only 1,200 or 1,500 are Chinese.

There is no cleanliness anywhere in the steppe. *Ch'ou Ta-tzŭ* ("foul Tartars") is a Chinese term of contempt hundreds of years old, and the justice of the reproach in the mouth of a race whose notions of sanitation are still rudimentary, is not at first apparent. At Urga a comparison is possible, and it is in favour of the Chinese. In the Mongol town hygiene, public or private, does not exist; there are some signs of it in Mai-mai-chên. It should not surprise us that Lamaistic monasticism is so unpleasant. The core of monasticism is a sense of the virtue of abstinence from worldly pleasures, and there was a time in the early Christian Church when purity of soul was held to be incompatible with washing of the body.

The Russian Consulate, known to Mongols as the "Green House", from the colour of the roof, dates from 1863. It occupies a commanding position midway between Mai-mai-chên and Mongol Urga, and is now supported by a large brick building, which contains the offices of the Russo-Chinese Bank and of a Russian mining company, and by the houses of a few Russian traders. Close by are the barracks which were improvised in haste for the 200 or 300 Cossacks sent in 1900 to protect the Russian community. Both Consulate and barracks were protected by a ditch filled with wire entanglements, which were intended to arrest night surprises; and though the situation was sufficiently acute in the autumn of 1900 to warrant these precautions, they were considered no longer necessary in 1902, and the bulk of the Cossack guard was under orders to withdraw to Siberia. I was given to understand that the sagacity of Mr Shishmarev, the Russian Consul-General, whose 40 years of peaceful service at Urga has secured him an influence of exceptional weight in the councils of the Lamaistic Hierarchy and Ambans, alone prevented the spread of the Boxer madness across the Gobi to the Chinese communities of North Mongolia.

## BOGDO UL: SACRED MOUNTAIN OF URGA

The Urga Valley is closed in by mountains, of which Bogdo Ul is the most remarkable. Fritsche put its absolute height at 5,412 feet—that is to say, 700 feet above Urga. It is the Han-shan (Khan-ul) of the Chinese, and is mentioned by Gaubil as the traditional burial place of Jinghis. There is no tradition of the sort nowadays. The respect paid by Mongols to conspicuous hills is no doubt a survival of pre-Buddhistic beliefs, but the chief cause of the reverence with which Bogdo Ul is now treated is the proximity of the Bogdo's residence. It is not permitted to anyone to hunt or fell trees on any portion of it and no execution should take place in sight of it. Criminals condemned to death must be sent across the Gobi to Dolon-nor or Kalgan.

Pozdnyéev mentions a memorial [report] of 1778, sent by the Mongol Amban to the Emperor Ch'ien-lung, in which it was alleged that Khan-ul owed its name (Khan's Mount) to the fact that Jinghis was born close by, and though the Chinese Court were aware that this was not so, they sanctioned the institution of seasonal sacrifices, which are continued at the present day. Every year in spring and autumn scented candles and silks are offered in sacrifice near the summit of the mountain, on dates fixed by the lamas, by the Princes of the Tushetu and Tsetsen Aimaks. To the traveller from China by the Kalgan route, Bogdo Ul is specially noteworthy on account of the thick covering of pine, Siberian larch, birch, mountain ash, and cedar with which it is covered, the first patch of forest to charm the eye after 600 miles of indifferent steppe vegetation.

## THE KENTEI MOUNTAINS

I had originally intended to continue on from Urga westward, through Uliasutai and Kobdo to Semipalatinsk, visiting the Orkhon Valley and the ancient Karakorum on the way—a long journey of 50 or 60 days' marching, but I was told on very good authority that I could scarcely hope to cross the Altais so late in the season without some serious walking, and an injury to a foot made this impossible. My attention was invited to the Kentei Mountains instead and, after arranging for the dispersal of my caravan and the return of the Indian sub-surveyor and Chinese servants to Peking, I made a rapid journey in a tarantass [a four-wheeled Russian vehicle mounted on poles] with Mr von Grot through Jun Khure to some gold mines on the Terelchi Gol, 150 miles north-east of Urga. The Terelchi is one of the feeders of the Upper Kerulon, and the gold mines here and on the Iro River (a tributary of the Selenga) are worked by a Russian company, which holds a monopoly of mining enterprise in the Tsetsen and Tushetu Khanates. Many of the valleys radiating from the Kentei range are auriferous [contain gold], and some are evidently rich enough in gold to repay the attention of capitalists. With the exception of gold-washings on the east slopes of the Southern Hingan, I neither saw nor heard of mineral products of any commercial importance until I reached the Kerulon.

A two-days' ride from the Terelchi gold mines along the Kerulon—now a shallow, stony stream of variable width, rapid and clear—through lone valleys which are marshy in summer and frozen during the remainder of the year, brought me to the foot of the Kentei *massif*. This is the holiest of the many holy mountains in Mongolia. Thither every autumn the Manchu Amban comes from Urga with a retinue of magnitude, to make oblation [an offering] to the great nature-spirits, and Mongols and Chinese alike make pilgrimages from great distances to enlist their favour.

## MOUNT KENTEI

Our camping place (4,500 feet) was strewn with the debris of fires, mutton bones, skeletons of camels, felled logs, and broken carts, relics of the yearly visits of the Urga Amban. I rode up through a thick forest of pine, larch, and cedar to the *dalai* (ocean), the sacred lakelet on the south slope of Kentei. It is an irregular oblong, 1,000 yards from east to west, by 300 to 400 yards, and approximating 5,600 feet above sea level. Of course, the Mongol guide (a pleasant lama friend of Mr von Grot) said that it was bottomless, but the water, though limpid, had not the dark azure of great depths. The shore is easily accessible on the east side; elsewhere the rocks rise steeply from the water's edge. Bleached drift-wood cumbered this east beach, and a large *obo* was formed of it, before which our lama prayed long and earnestly, and burnt a paper invocation. He also drank some of the water, which is credited with therapeutic qualities of supernatural origin. I have seldom felt the charm of a scene so much, and I noticed that both my companions—the lama and a matter-of-fact Chinese soldier—were unusually silent and contemplative.

Next morning (21st September) we mounted to the summit of Kentei. At 7 am in our camp the thermometer stood at 29 degrees [Fahrenheit], but as we emerged on the exposed ridge above, a strong nor'-wester drove it down to 17 degrees, and the crests of the higher hills were veiled with snow. In half-an-hour we reached the main altar, where the Amban worships. In front of a large tree *obo*, festooned with prayer flags, there are rough tables of larch, with a boarding in front, on which the Amban kneels, and before this again there was a large earthenware cauldron full of *airak* (fermented mare's milk). Our lama stirred the *airak* with a pole, and produced from the depths remains of *hatakh* (scarf-offerings), walnuts, and tea-leaves. Close by the cauldron, on the top of a small stone pile, I noticed some clay masks, open-jawed, of conspicuously evil expression. The ground was covered with walnuts, cheese *hatakh*, and Tibetan prayers, written on calico and on paper. The lama prostrated himself thrice at full-length before the *obo*, and added a rag to it; the Chinese guard contented himself with one prostration and an offering of a piece of bread, which he placed at the foot of the tree. On my return journey I disturbed a capercaillie [large, turkey-like grouse], who was feeding on the walnuts around this altar and, secure in the prohibition against shooting on the sacred mountain, he perched on a branch close by and watched me take some photographs.

The summit (6,600 feet) was reached without difficulty, except for the wind. The pilgrimages of centuries have marked recognizable paths, and Mongols ride the whole way up over tree-roots and fallen trunks. The slope was forested, but the broad uneven crest was blown bare of trees, and its surface was a mass of large loose stones of irregular shapes. When approaching the mountain, I observed from a distance of 6 miles a rounded *boss* [rocky protuberance] on the summit, which had been mentioned to me by Mr von Grot. I clambered over this, and found it to be an oval tumulus, 250 yards long, east and west, and 200 yards north and south, of the same loose stones which cover the mountain. I had no doubt that it was a human creation. There are two large stone *obos* on the crest of the tumulus, and on one of them there were the remains of a bronze censer [incense burner]. From a fragment of a Manchu inscription on this, which I copied, M. Dolbejev, of the Russian Consulate at Urga, read the date of the 12th year of Ch'ien-lung (AD 1748).

## The tomb of Jinghis

This is a remarkable tumulus, probably the largest in Mongolia. I am unable to believe that it is merely a prayer cairn, and it is a conjecture of Mr von Grot, which, I think, is entitled to attention, that we have here the veritable tomb of Jinghis. Though we are informed that the body of Jinghis was borne secretly from the north of Shansi, where he died (AD 1227), into Mongolia, and that the guards killed every one they met "*sur cette longue route*" ["on this long road"] to prevent the news of his death spreading prematurely, there is no indication that the place of burial (as distinct from the actual grave) was kept a secret, and it is remarkable that it is not definitely known to Mongols. It is true that Potanin discovered in 1884, in the north-east corner of the Ordos country, a shrine composed of two felt tents and some wooden huts, which is said locally to mark the "remains" of Jinghis; but this appears to be a merely local belief at variance with all the earlier records. D'Ohsson, on the authority of Raschid (who wrote 70 or 80 years after the death of Jinghis), says that Jinghis was buried

> *sur l'une des montagnes qui forment la chaîne du Bourcan–Caldoun, d'où sortent les fleuves Onon, Kéroulan, et Toula* [on one of these mountains, part of the Bourcan–Caldoun chain, from which flow the Onon, Kéroulan, and Toula rivers]

and he concludes that

> *on peut admettre comme certain d'après le témoignage de Raschid, de Marco Polo, et de Gaubil, que Tchinguiz-Khan et plusieurs Princes de sa dynastie furent enterrés près des sources de l'Onon et du Kéroulan.* [one has to conclude, following the evidence of Raschid, Marco Polo and Gaubil, that Tchinguiz-Khan and several princes of his dynasty are buried near the sources of the Onon and the Kéroulan.]

In a note to his translation of a portion of Raschid, Quatremère says:

> *Il me parait donc bien démontré que la montagne de Bourkhan–Kaldoun est identique avec celle que les Manchous appellent Hanalin (la montagne de Han ou de Kan) et que le P. Gerbillon désigne sous le nom de Kentey.*

[It seems quite obvious that the mountain of
Bourkhan–Kaldoun is identical with that which the
Manchous call Hanalin (the mountain of Han or
Kan) and which Gerbillon calls Kentey.]

Ssanang Setzen names the burial-place "Yakeh Utek,
between the north slope of the Altai Khan and the
south slope of Kentei Khan," and, in his description of
the funeral, mentions that the two-wheeled cart bearing the coffin stuck in the "blue clay soil" (this would
point to the marshy valleys of the Upper Kerulon),
and that a mound was raised over the grave. The official Yüan history places the interment on Mount
Kinien, north of the Gobi, which was also the sepul-
chre of Jinghis's successors. Gaubil remarks that the
position of Mount Kinien is not stated exactly in this
history, but he adds

> *plusieurs Seigneurs* Mongous *de la famille de Gentchiscan
> ont dit ici [Peking] que Gentchiscan est enterré sur la
> montagne de* Han—*Montagne* Han, *lat. 47° 54'; long.
> 9° 3' occident.* [several members of the Gentchiscan
> family have said that Gentichiscan is buried on the
> Mountain of Han.]

To me it seems that Mount Kentei is indicated.
The possible alternative is the Bogdo Ul closing the
Urga Valley on the south, still called Han-shan (Khan-
Ul, the Han Alin of d'Anville's map) by the Chinese,
on the crest of which there is also a tumulus of some
dimensions.

There is a curious analogy between the Kentei Shan and Paik-tu San, the sacred mountain of North Korea. On the flanks of both, three rivers take their rise—Tumen, Yalu, and Sungari on Paik-tu San; Onon, Kerulon, and Tola on Kentei—there are holy lakes near the summits of both, and both are revered officially. These official obeisances in the case of Kentei are performed on the slope of the mountain, but the Korean officials are content to worship their "ancestral mountain" from the first point of vision, which is probably 70 miles off.

## RETURN TO URGA VIA THE TOMB OF TONYUKUK

I returned rapidly to the Terelchi mines and Urga, and on the 27th September visited, in company with M. Evstiféyev, a Russian acquaintance who is well versed in Siberian archaeology, the tomb of Tonyukuk (Tonjukuk). Of the antique remains of North Mongolia I first saw signs near Para-hota in a much-worn granite monolith which I examined in vain for inscriptions. Ancient barrows, called *kereksur*, are numerous in the hilly country from Kentei westward to the Altais, but Tonyukuk's tomb is in a class by itself. It lies in a broad open valley called Bain Sukht, 8 miles south of the Tola, and an easy day's ride, say 30 miles, from Urga. The monuments cover a space of 50 yards by 40. At the east end are two upright rudely squared stones, covered with old Turkish inscriptions in a wonderfully complete state. These have been deciphered by Radlov, and the history of Tonyukuk, an old Turkish hero who flourished in the seventh century, has been pieced together from Chinese sources by Professor Hirth. At the west end there is an altar (?) 10 feet square, formed of flat stones resting on edge, which at one time supported two similar stones placed horizontally. In the centre of the top stones a centre hole was cut, and the vertical slabs are ornamented by curved patterns engraved with a chisel. Beside this altar was a smaller one of similar structure, and between it and the two monoliths a variety of rude stone figures, mutilated and headless, were lying about. From the tomb eastward there ran, for 1,500 yards, a single straight row of some 300 unhewn rough stones, stuck upright in the ground, each of which is supposed to represent a fallen enemy.

This tomb was only discovered a few years ago by Madame Klementz, the wife of the well-known Siberian archaeologist, who ran across it in the course of her botanical excursions, and, fortunately, was alive to the importance of the inscriptions. When I reached this remarkable monument, which stands prominently on swelling ground 2 miles from the base of the higher hills, I could not help reflecting on the curious fact that two scientific expeditions, the Finnish of 1890, and the Russian of 1891, specially equipped for archaeological researches, had spent some days at Urga, and a score of other scientific and inquiring travellers had passed within a few miles, without hearing of its existence. It is a striking illustration of the narrow circle within which information on any Mongol antiquity is obtainable, and should be an incentive to further leisurely and systematic search.

# THE ORKHON VALLEY AND
# ERDENI TSU (KARAKORUM)

I spent the greater part of October in another rapid expedition to the Orkhon River and Erdeni Tsu in company with M. Evstiféyev. The wide valley of this great affluent of the Selenga abounds in luxuriant pastures, the great attraction for nomads, and it is safe to conclude, from the many monuments and ruins which have been discovered of late years, that this favoured region was the centre of the old Turkish and

Uigur dominions, as it was the headquarters of Ogotai [son of Jinghis] and his immediate successors. Since Yadrintsev discovered, in 1885, the bilingual monuments (Chinese and old Turkish) in honour of the last great Turkish Khan, Mogilan, and his brother Kultegin, two scientific expeditions have examined this neighbourhood, and the results have been published by the Finno-Ugrian Society of Helsingfors, and by the Russian Imperial Academy of Sciences. The great finds, of course, were the long inscriptions in an unknown writing, of which some fragmentary specimens had been found in the Yenesci Valley from the days of Messerschmidt. With the new material obtained from the tombs of Kultegin and Mogilan, Professor Thomson of Copenhagen was able to supply the key which Radlov applied, and we now know the purpose of these inscriptions. They confirm the national Turkish traditions which Raschid and Jowaini have handed down from lost Uigur books, that the valleys of the Orkhon and Upper Selenga were the original home of the Turks.

I must sound a note of warning with regard to the tomb of Kultegin. The local Mongols received orders in 1896 or 1897 from the Chinese Government to preserve the Chinese inscription (the Chinese inscription is on one side of the stone, and the Turkish is on the reverse side), and when I visited the tomb on the 15th October, it was sheltered by a solid brick-and-tile structure of Chinese pattern. Unfortunately, the walls are built up to the sides of the memorial stone, the joints between it and the walls are cemented, and it is now impossible to examine the Turkish inscription, which, of course, must suffer in damp seasons by being boxed up in this fashion. It was especially irritating to see that the workmen sent to construct this shelter had obtained their basement course of grey granite by chiselling 2 feet off the side of an enormous sacrificial stone or plinth.

The turning-point of my Orkhon journey was Erdeni Tsu, which is marked on the old Jesuit maps as Erdeni Chao. Erdeni Tsu was the first Lamaistic shrine established in the Khalha Khanates and, according to Mongol records which have been translated by Pozdnyéev, it was founded in 1586 in the city which had been the residence of Jinghis's son Ogotai—that is to say, in the old Mongol capital, Karakorum. The existing monastery—which, if it is overshadowed politically by those of Urga, is still the most venerated of Mongolian holy places—is a collection of temples and shrines enclosed by a square of mud walls, 500 yards on the side and 15 feet high. It lies on the north slope of low bare hills, but westward the view is bounded by the forested ridges of the Khangai range. The walls, as usual, face the cardinal points; there is a large gate in the centre of each, and white dagobas (*sobergha*), built at intervals of 20 to 25 yards, take the place of bastions. There are a number of old monumental stones with inscriptions—Chinese, Arabic, and Mongol—which the Radlov expedition examined, but I was most interested by the uneven space north and north-east of the monastery walls. There one finds an area of three-quarters of a square mile covered with irregular mounds, which attract notice at once as not being natural.

Walking over this I observed pieces of tiles, broken bricks, and occasional lumps of granite, which showed traces of the chisel. At first I thought, seeing a number of refuse heaps scattered about, that these bricks and tiles might have been deposited in the course of the last 300 years by the inhabitants of the monastery, but I had opportunities of assuring myself that they were really independent remains of old buildings. A portion of one of the mounds had been worn at the side by cart traffic, and another had been excavated recently; and in the exposed parts I saw bricks and tiles, whole and broken, embedded in the earth in a manner to banish all doubt. This area is the site of an ancient town which has been covered by aerial action, assisted by a yearly thatch of dwarf artemisia and grasses.

At a mile-and-a-half to the north of the monastery I struck a *balgas*, running east and west for 1,200 paces, and north and south again for 800 paces. Karakorum undoubtedly lay in this part of the Orkhon Valley, and though Paderin was under the justifiable impression when, in 1873, he visited Khara-balgas, which is 20 miles north of Erdeni Tsu and is now believed to have been the headquarters of an Uigur King, that he had found the site of Ogotai's capital, the evidence of the Erdenin Erikhe produced by Pozdnyéev, and the existence of the ruins I have roughly described above, make it more than probable that Erdeni Tsu is the real site. If the Mongols could be won from their present rabid opposition to archaeological delving, it might be possible to change this probability into a certainty.

# KARAKORUM TO LONDON

From Erdeni Tsu I turned eastward to Urga, and thence northward to Kiakhta, making a detour to the Iro gold mines on my way. The country between Urga and Kiakhta has often been described. It is quite distinct from the arid Mongolian plateau. Close to Urga the line of heights which limit the basin of the Siberian rivers is crossed, and there is a gradual descent through forested hills and well-watered valleys.

Kiakhta is still the leading emporium of the North Mongol trade, but its importance has been sadly diminished by the construction of the Siberian and Manchurian Railways. From 1727 to 1860 it was the sole legitimate outlet for Russo-Chinese commerce in the whole of the north portion of Mongolia, and the annual winter fairs were then almost as famous as those of Nijni Novgorod. One hears little of these fairs nowadays. The huge custom-house built to accommodate the enormous quantities of tea which were transported across the Gobi until quite recently was empty, many of the merchants' houses in Kiakhta proper were untenanted, and the decline of the place was the subject of general lamentation. Troitskosavsk, the Russian district town 5 versts★ north of Kiakhta, has also suffered from the diversion of the tea trade, and I gathered from a conversation with a Chinese trader that the Chinese Mai-mai-chên, which is just across the frontier from Kiakhta, shares deeply in the general depression.

From Kiakhta I travelled by the Russian post road through Selenginsk. Nearing Verkhne Udinsk I was arrested by heavy snow, and the Selenga being impassable from ice-floes, I took to a sleigh and caught the Siberian mail train at the little station of Tataurova on the morning of the 8th November. Irkutsk was reached on the 9th November and, by leisurely stages, Moscow on the 21st November, St Petersburgh on the 25th November, and London on the 2nd December.

---

★ A Russian measure of length, about 0.66 mile.

# OBSERVATIONS ON THE PEOPLE, LIFE, TRADE, AND PRODUCTS

## THE MONGOL PEOPLE

The typical Mongol is a short squat person, with a round (*brachycephalic*) head, a broad face much sun-burnt, yellowish skin, black oblique eyes, black hair worn Chinese fashion in a pigtail (lamas, of course, are shaven), and a flat nose. It is a hardy race, but unused to careful labour of any kind, and incapable at present of continuous attention or exertion. I had heard much of Mongol simplicity, but I met little of it. There is no keener or more tenacious bargainer than a Mongol, and truth does not enter into his code.

I was told that woman holds a very inferior position in Mongolia, but I could not satisfy myself that this was so. The life she leads is inferior in Mongol estimation: milking, cooking, needlework and felt-making are less agreeable occupations than the eternal gadding about on horseback, herding or visiting, in which the men pass most of their time. There is little scope for the display of feminine qualities, nor does the nomadic life foster these. There is nothing radiant about the Mongol woman; with rare exceptions she is withered and slattern [dirty], or young and slattern. Not even the daughters of princes can be said to "exist beautifully". No doubt the legal position of the wife in a family is an inferior one, at any rate, so long as her mother-in-law is alive, but her actual place and influence depend on herself.

A European cannot see much of the country without noticing the great freedom of intercourse between the two sexes. The movements and actions of the women are, from the character of the life, completely untrammelled by the conventions to which we are accustomed. Women and girls making journeys on horseback, or in carts, alone or in the company of men not their kinsmen, were to be met with commonly; our tents were visited by merry wives and maids eager to inspect the stranger's belongings, and they sat down as a matter of course in the circle of our Mongol henchmen, and were in no way preoccupied by their own innocence. Husbands and fathers are constantly absent from their tents, sometimes for long periods, leaving the wives and daughters to look after themselves.

Marriage has no religious significance. It is a civil contract, whose binding force is the mere will of the parties. The husband or the wife seems to be at liberty to dissolve it for any reason that appears good to him or her, and there is no restriction on the re-marriage of either. Monogamy is the ideal basis of the family, such as this is in Mongolia; but in practice it is not allowed to interfere with polygamous experiments when the means to indulge in these are not wanting. Glaring irregularity in these matters is held in check by the fear of exciting interference from the wife's relations, and then a woman divorced takes her dowry and personal property with her. But there is little or no moral censure of concubinage. I once came across a Mongol lady with two husbands (she was the best man of the three), and though the *ménage* was considered unusual there was no social condemnation.

No official figures of the population have ever been published to my knowledge. The most reliable estimate I have seen places the number of Mongols in Inner and Outer Mongolia at 5,000,000; but whatever the population, according to all the information I could gather, it is declining. In a country peopled by an indigenous race which has not been disturbed politically for two centuries, this is a notable fact.

Lamaistic monasticism is partly responsible for it, though a large percentage of the lamas I came across are married, rear families, live away from their monasteries, and pursue the callings of Mongol laymen. The infant mortality is large, especially in North Mongolia, where the climatic conditions are least favourable to the nomadic life, and there is scarcely a doubt that disease is on the increase.

Before the Mongols under Jinghis began campaigning against the world, they were addicted to the species of internecine squabbles which we associate with the civilization of the American Indian. They were predatory and aggressive, and perforce [inevitably] worked off superabundant energy in inter-tribal conflicts until they waxed strong enough to undertake distant forays against external societies. This combative activity remained a characteristic long after the decline of the Mongol dominion in Asia, and so far as Mongolia proper is concerned, its subsidence synchronizes roughly with the rise of the Manchus in China. The Mongol of today, if not a thoroughly peaceable creature, has lost the old fierce predatory instinct, and the fight in his blood finds sufficient vent in horse races and wrestling matches. Why is it? One might reasonably infer that the change was due to Manchu suppression if it were not well known that the Manchu yoke has been light. It is scarcely conceivable that the trifling amount of control applied could have crushed so sharply and completely the instincts which moved the race to momentous conquests only three centuries before. For the altering influences we have to look amongst the Mongols themselves, and the simplicity of their lives ought to make the search a short one.

If we glance at the material environment of the Mongol, and compare it with that described by Rubruquis less than 30 years after Jinghis died, there are no striking differences to chronicle. The average man eats, drinks, and dresses today very much as his forebears ate, drank, and dressed. His droves and herds pasture on the same lands, and are tended in the same primitive fashion. If a Mongol of AD 1200 were brought to life he would probably find that the tent and household utensils are not quite what he was accustomed to, and yet he would have small difficulty in assigning to each strange article its proper use. It is likely, however, that he would require more explanation with regard to the *Borhan*—the little Buddhistic shrine which takes a prominent place in every tent— than about anything else, and it would probably take him some time to square his actions with the spiritual and ethical notions which have followed in the train of the new gods. Our resuscitated Mongol would, indeed, discover that the religious *milieu* was widely different from that in which he had grown up. He would notice that instead of a few Shamanist sorcerers, who were probably no more numerous relatively than priests are in our communities, at least one-third of his countrymen had devoted themselves to spiritual things; that this one-third lived a form of life in magnificent buildings and underwent a mental discipline which to him was exceedingly strange; that these monks acted with a solidity and astuteness which made them the social authority in the land; and that this powerful organization, however unscrupulous it might be in serving its own material interests, preached a religion of lenity [gentleness] and piety, of arrest of passion and submission to fate, as different in essentials from the mysticism of his day as light from darkness.

This dominant ecclesiasticism is, then, the great social factor which distinguishes the old Mongol society from the modern. We know that it came from Tibet in the declining period of the Ming dynasty, and that its influence was already notable by the time the Manchus came to deal with Mongolia. They saw at once that it was the only organization which was not limited by tribal divisions; that its whole teaching was peace; that the weight of its interests must lean to peace; that the celibacy of so large a proportion of the male population must relieve the pressure for existence and make for peace; and they moulded their policy accordingly. The Lamaistic Church has been recognized, supported, and, when necessary, controlled with a solicitude quite foreign to the methods of the Chinese Government in China proper, and the result of this policy has been a curious equilibrium of the social forces and a tempering of the natural disposition which seems to have removed the Mongols from the list of aggressive races.

## FOOD AND AGRICULTURE

The native larder is usually restricted to products of the dairy, mutton, and brick tea [tea pressed into cakes]. Wherever the Chinaman penetrates, and that is pretty well everywhere nowadays, parched millet or barley, or wheat or oat flour, goes with him, and becomes a fairly common article of diet. All manner of flesh, including carrion, is eaten on occasion, but the staple meat is mutton; beef is slaughtered on festive occasions only, horse or camel flesh are not thought of until the animals are moribund, unless under pressure of exceptional circumstances. Poultry never appears in the bill of fare, fish almost never (I met with ichthyophagus [fish-eating] Mongols on the north shore of Bur Nor only), wild fowl and feathered game rarely or never, though the ponds and lakes teem in season, and North Mongolia swarms with sand grouse. The meat of predilection, when it can be got, is antelope, in which the Mongols show signs of a palate; along the Kerulon and Orkhon the *tarbukh* (*Arctomys bobac*) [type of marmot] is pursued relentlessly for fur and flesh; but the hare is despised.

Vegetables, fruit, pastry, sweets, and spices are unknown in the indigenous cuisine; dried jujubes (*Zizyphus*), Tibet raisins, candy and Chinese confections occur only on the tables of the rich. There is no notion of the art of cookery. That tea shall boil and that meat shall at least be heated through are the two simple rules of the Mongol housewife. Mutton is eaten as soon as it is killed, except in winter, and you will hear adverse comments if the sheep is small, but none on its toughness. The Mongol wields a strong jaw and good teeth, but he hurries over his meat, which is usually as hard as leather, and perforce bolts it.

I saw comparatively little true desert along my route, and in any case I should say that want of water and not a naturally inhospitable soil is responsible for the scanty steppe vegetation. Failure of the monsoon showers in July is rarely general, but when it is, pastures are few and far between and distress is widespread. The state of the grass is the constant topic, and one experience of a drought-stricken region is enough to impress upon the traveller the importance to these nomads of the few running streams and permanent pastures which they possess.

As agriculture withdraws land from the general pastures to which all have rights, it is forbidden. I never saw anything but the merest cabbage and onion bed cultivated by Mongols. Farming is carried on with much success by the Chinese, who have (by the exercise of dextrous and palm-greasing diplomacy) acquired land, both in South-East Mongolia and along the Siberian frontier (valleys of the Upper Selenga and its tributaries), and no doubt there are considerable tracts in the river valleys of North Mongolia which could produce excellent crops of oats, pulse, and potatoes.

## MECHANICAL INDUSTRIES

There is very little mechanical industry of any sort. Almost everything the Mongol wears, and nearly all his metal utensils, come from China or Siberia. Mongol blacksmiths and silversmiths exist, but their work is of the rudest, and though most Mongols can handle the few tools necessary for the construction of tent frames and country carts, none appear to have the smallest notion of building. The temples are all the work of Chinese, and when repairs are necessary Chinese masons and labourers have to be imported, sometimes from a distance of 500 miles. Even the sheepskins for winter robes are now cured by itinerant Chinese tanners, and I have met Chinese dyers who plied their craft in the summer months, passing from tent to tent for hundreds of miles. Felt appears to be the one article which is still made regularly in every *ail*, and remarkably good felt it is.

## DOMESTIC ANIMALS

Cattle and stock-breeding is practically the sole legitimate occupation of all Mongols, and the animal of first importance is the pony. He is the commonest of possessions, the everyday means of locomotion, and the staple topic of conversation. The Mongol who walks is indeed poor, for he must be friendless as well as moneyless. A man who does not own a pony is rarely refused the use of one from a neighbour's drove, and a comparative stranger will ask for the loan of a mount in much the same way as a European will turn to a passer-by for a match. From early childhood the Mongol acquires the habit of scrambling on the back of the nearest pony to cover any distance over a few yards, and anyone who has tried a Mongol boot for pedestrian purposes will understand his reluctance to walk a step when he can be carried. The outdoor life of both sexes and of all ages is spent on horseback, and the aspect of a Mongol on foot usually reminded me of the story told of Michaelangelo: after 22 months of painting the ceiling of the Sistine Chapel he got so used to looking upward that he lost the faculty of looking straight before him, and had to hold his book outstretched above his head when he wanted to read. The Mongol always walks as if he had to consult the movements of a pony under him.

## The Mongol pony

A good specimen of the Mongol pony is perhaps the best of his size in the world for general use. The head and shoulders will be too heavy for elegance, the eyes none too full, the muzzle and crest coarse, and the manners too often objectionable, but the quarters, loins, and legs are good, the barrel deep and long, and there is no deficiency of bone. European residents on the China coast have used Mongol ponies in number during the past half century for all purposes—hacking, racing, chasing, and harness work—and the common opinion held is that they are great weight carriers, and capable of an exceptional amount of work at moderate pressure. Reared in the open steppe, with little or no human care, they are accustomed to great extremes of weather and thrive on the coarsest forage. I rode a six-year-old Mongol pony from Peking (June 3rd) to the Kerulon (August 30th), a distance of 1,300 miles, through many stretches of bad or inferior pasture, and beyond a slight temporary lameness caused by hobbles [fetters], he was neither sick nor sorry at any time. When I parted with him he was worn and thin, but quite sound, and capable of carrying me for another fortnight. Once beyond the China border he received no stall provender [fodder], and was simply turned loose at halts to pick up what he could. For mounted infantry purposes in wild countries there is no more useful animal.

The size and character vary with the locality. The commonest colour is grey, chestnut follows, and then come bay and sorrel. Stallions are selected animals, especially in North Mongolia, but the mares are not, and no special pains are taken anywhere to improve a breed. Along the China border the ponies are undersized, 12 to 13 hands, the result of the incessant demands of the China markets for all the larger beasts. As one travels northward, and the China markets become more remote, the horseflesh improves (12.2 to 14 hands), and the best specimens of the Mongol pony are found in the valley of the Kerulon. Prices are unstable, but the average cost of a well-shaped 13-hand pony in 1900 was in the neighbourhood of 3*l*.

According to my Mongol servants there are only three serious diseases affecting ponies—glanders, mange, and "staggers". In the case of glanders isolation is practised, and in all three prompt sale to the Man-tzu (Chinese) is recommended as the best specific [remedy].

## The Mongol camel

The camel comes a good second to the pony in point of general usefulness, though far inferior in number. I have heard the number of ponies in Mongolia estimated at 5,000,000, and I fancy that this is not too optimistic a figure, but there can scarcely be more than one-tenth of that number of camels. The Mongol camel is the Bactrian or two-humped species; he is larger than the Arabian, accustomed to much greater extremes of weather, and to the coarsest and scantiest provender [fodder].

I saw little camel-breeding in Chabaria; there was more in the Hingan region; in the Khalha country camel droves were most numerous. Opinions vary, but a cameleer of wide experience told me that the best animals he had to deal with came from the east side of the Hingan Mountains, the next best and little inferior, were from the Khalha Khanates, and the worst hailed from Kuei-hua-ch'êng and West Mongolia. The last are tall and weedy and least hardy. Large feet and squat broad figures are the characteristics of the more useful camels, and when in condition the humps are always upright, fat, and firm.

The price varies greatly. My camels were picked and cost 5*l.* 5*s.* each at Kalgan; at Urga similar animals could be purchased for 3*l*. or less. The best are bought by the Chinese for the coal traffic south of the Great Wall, and they cost up to 8*l*. or 10*l*. in Peking.

For three months, I watched our camels daily, and though one could never take the interest in any one of them that is natural as regards ponies, it seemed to me that their character was maligned by common Chinese opinion. They gave us singularly little trouble. There were two or three stampedes, and a half-a-dozen cases of individual beasts deliberately discarding their loads in the early part of the journey, for the camel is easily startled and occasionally frisky, but as time wore on the loads were accepted with patient resignation. It is the uniform pessimistic look which prejudices against the camel, and the grating grunt or squeal, which is his usual protest, is not a pleasant sound.

The average load of my camels during the whole journey was over 300 lbs; these loads were borne from Khara-usu to Urga, 1,270 miles, in 62 marching days, and at the end there was no serious alteration in condition. And I should add that my mode of travel was not the best for camels. Mongol caravans journey much at night, to avoid working in the heat of the day, and because camels will not feed in the dark; but as my object was to see the country and not merely cover ground, I had to travel very often in the torrid hours. I know no animal who can eat so voraciously and so quickly as the camel, and he refuses nothing that he can masticate. He prefers objectionable water, especially if it has a strong dash of soda in it, and he enjoys the wild onion so much that it is always advisable to ride to windward of him. Though there is comparatively little true desert in Mongolia, water is nearly always a preoccupation, and in Central Mongolia and the Gobi there are many routes which only camels can take without risk, because of their ability to go three days or more without water.

## Cattle and sheep

Cattle breeding is universal. The commonest of sights was a line of calves tethered in front of a tent awaiting the return of the cows from pasture. The breed resembles our Highland cattle, and though the coat is not so shaggy it is equally hardy. The very minimum of care is taken of cattle, and they are generally in poor condition. Oxen are employed for draught purposes throughout the country, and great numbers are sold across the Siberian frontier and to the Chinese of Manchuria, but the main check on the increase of horned stock is rinderpest, which occurs frequently.

The sheep are all of the fat-tailed variety, and their number is legion; there is scarcely a family without a drove. They are the "most profitablest cattle" to the Mongol, for without their wool, skins, and flesh it is hard to imagine how he could get through the steppe winters. The average price of a three-year-old sheep in 1902 was something under 4s.; in large droves they were purchasable readily for 2s. 6d. or 3s. a head. Neither pigs nor poultry are kept by Mongols; I missed the fowls, but the character of the Eastern pig early drives one to the adoption of Mahommedan prejudices.

The yak (*Bos grunniens*), here called *sarlik*, is kept in the place of cattle to a considerable extent throughout the mountainous parts of North Mongolia. I came across him first on the Upper Kerulon, where he is used for draught purposes. Hybrids of the yak and ordinary cattle are common, and their milk is much esteemed.

## PASTIMES

### Racing

Racing is the national pastime. It is in the main a warm weather sport. From May to August pony races are the attraction at the temple festivals and fairs, and most considerable owners train a selection from their speediest ponies for the local meetings. A racing stud of dimensions commensurate with rank and wealth is the proper appanage [status symbol] of a prince or *Jassak*, and his "string" usually includes some of the fastest beasts of the district. Nearing the Tsetsen Khan's palace, I observed tethered to two long lines in the open steppe, some 40 ponies of all ages, from two-year-olds upwards; this is the most renowned racing stable in Mongolia. But any Mongol who is fortunate enough to possess a noted galloper, and is rich enough in horseflesh to spare his services during the training period, is pretty certain to race him. And this national sport is as little affected by money indelicacies as any that I know of. I constantly heard of matches between rival owners proud of the reputation of their stock, but seldom of serious betting on the result. There are prizes to winners, rarely of tempting value. In the Chahar country the stakes are usually an ounce or two of silver (say, 2*s.* 6*d.* or 5*s.*) for a race of 10 miles, but now and then an opulent magnate has occasion to be generous, and offers something exceptional—cattle, sheep, or ponies, silk or clothes. I was told that the competition was always keen, no matter what the prize, and the gossip telegraph of the steppe assures winners of a reputation curiously tenacious and widespread. The races are never under 10 miles long; the "Derby" of Mongolia, which takes place near Urga, under the direct patronage of the Bogdo, is a contest over 30 miles of rough steppe. A special feature about this classic race is that all the winners are presented to the Bogdo, who maintains them for the rest of their lives in honourable idleness.

## A race meeting in Chaharia

In July 1899 I rode over with Mr Larsen from my camp at Khara-usu to a temple at Haliutai, close by Angul Nor in Chaharia, to witness a race meeting. It was a characteristic gathering, and a sketch of it may give a more definite impression of South Mongol society and amusements than much general description. A line of eleven large blue tents crested a wave of the plain, a short way east of the temple; they belonged to Chahar officials and local notables (all have rank if not office), most of whom were directly interested in the horse-race. These tents were ranged some 100 yards or more behind a square blue cotton pavilion, which sheltered a cushioned daïs [raised table] for the reception of the local *gegen* [religious leader]; to right and left of the daïs were rows of tiny tables and cushions spread on the ground. In front of the pavilion, again three tents were set up so as to enclose a lozenge of turf some 60 yards in the side, the wrestling plot. The space between the line of tents and the pavilion swarmed with lamas and "black men" [laymen] in official garb, a few Chinese of disagreeable aspect and no ostensible occupation sidling amongst them, and all were examining or discussing the ponies which stood tethered or knee-haltered a few paces away from the tent doors.

No sooner had we dismounted than we were invited into one of the largest tents by the owner, an acquaintance of Mr Larsen. Our host was a well-to-do, neat man, of manners too elaborate for an unsophisticated Chahar. His tent, roomy and cool, was floored with a layer of rush-matting, strips of felt, and wool cushions in the bright reds and yellows so loved by Mongols. A crescent of cushion seats faced the entrance and I was shown to the place of honour. Before me lay a multi-coloured queridon of Jehol marquetry, a low table covered with garish American oil-cloth, and a dominating patch of inferior English carpet. Our host was evidently progressive, for I noticed on some occasion or other that he consulted a smart gilt-edged pocket book in red morocco [goat-skin leather] which was sedulously [carefully] interred in a cardboard box of frivolous exterior. In the light of the doorway a brawny lama son was in the hands of a diffident Chinese barber, who lamented the bluntness of the lama's razor; another son, a child of 10, promenaded solemnly in an official hat bearing a lately purchased button of the same rank as his father; and two other boys, grandchildren, contemplated their uncle raptly. Pressed curds, the mildest forms of cheese, and refreshing Chinese tea, were served to us. Soon two lamas of consequence from the Haliutai temple called formally, and our host rose, momentarily exchanged snuff-bottles, and bowed repeatedly, pushing them all the while into seats above him. They offered the conventional resistance before sitting, sipped a cup of tea, exchanged a few banalities about herds and the weather prospects, and took their way to another tent, our host leading to the door where he merely faced them for a moment as they left.

Towards noon the *gegen's* cavalcade approached over the plain from the Lamasery [monastery]. He sat in a Chinese springless cart upholstered in a quiet and superior style, which was drawn by two sedate, well-groomed mules, and escorted by mounted lamas clothed and hatted in glittering yellow satin. A knot of lay understrappers [junior officials], a body of police in sombre plum robes and gilt or white-buttoned hats, were in close attendance to fend off the curious, but there was no difficulty whatever in

keeping the *gegen* in full view without fear of offence.
He was a cheery-faced youth of eleven, who kept his
eyes roving intelligently, laughed silently and pleas-
antly whenever he was amused, which was often,
inhaled his bowl of tea with all the noise of a
Mongol, but never spoke, although he was often spoken to, and the conversation of his suite was loud and
free. Bands of servitors [servants] brought tray-tables
and dishes of muddy cakes daubed with carmine (a
lucky colour) from the ecclesiastical kitchen, a frowsy
blue tent, and set them before him as soon as he was
seated, and close upon their heels came a succession
of the prominent men at the gathering who donned
official robes to make their bow to His Grandeur.
Lamas squatted in two rows on the left side of the
pavilion, the laity gravitated to the right, and all drank
tea, chatted, and laughed with no apparent heed of
the presence of a celestial "incarnation".

Shortly after 1 o'clock the race ponies paraded in
front of the *gegen*'s pavilion, which was both starting
point and winning post, and at the moment I could
not help reflecting that a race-meeting with a bishop
in the judge's box, a public chiefly clerical, no book-
makers or betting, and nominal prizes, would be in
England the closest analogue of the odd spectacle.
The entries were all made at the post, and there were
no conditions of age or weight or owner's qualifica-
tion. I was told that I could join in the race if I
wished, and but for the atrocious length of it I should
have sent a race pony which I had with me, feeling
moderately certain from an inspection of the starters

that none of them were even second class in point of speed. The names of owners and descriptions of ponies were jotted down on a scrap of paper by a perambulating clerk, and at 1.23 pm the field, twelve in all, straggled at a walk in the direction of Chagan-balgas.

It cost me an effort to understand that this was the "start". Manes were decorated with strips of coloured silk, the long tails were bound in the middle by half-a-dozen coils of red cord, and the bridles, single snaffles with raw-hide reins, were each embellished by a round disk of burnished silver attached to the head band. The jockeys were the smallest boys capable of riding the distance which the owners could secure and, from the lamentations of one lama owner, whose pony finished a bad fourth, I gathered that there is a light-weight jockey difficulty in Mongolia as else-where in the world. I estimated the weight of the lightest urchin at between three and four stone, and the biggest boy could not have weighed less than 80 or 85 lbs. Some sported jackets of red or blue silk or chintz, but colours were not obligatory. A saddle or seat aid in any form was not allowed; the jockeys sim-ply rolled up their loose cotton trousers as high as they could and clutched the ponies' ribs with bare legs. All carried long whips. The course was not marked out in any way. It was understood to be a direct line from the *gegen*'s tent to the Kiakhta–Kalgan telegraph line, a distance of 20 *li* (over 6 miles) and back; and though it soon passed out of sight over the rolling steppe, which is peculiarly deficient in guiding features, no one seemed to find it difficult to keep straight. The 20 *li* outward were walked, and on arrival at the turning point the ponies were brought into line and sent on the return journey at a gallop. The winning pony reached the *gegen*'s tent 300 yards in front of the second, at 3.52 pm. In the 2½ hours taken up by this "race" only 13 miles of steppe were covered, a performance in no way remarkable, and the absence of weight conditions made it a fallacious test of the relative merits of the ponies. At no time in the race did I observe any faster pace than a three-quarter speed gallop, and only two or three of the ponies were completely exhausted at the finish.

## Wrestling

While the race was in progress pairs of wrestlers appeared in the "lozenge" in front of the *gegen*'s tent, and occupied the public attention. It was always a layman against a lama, a tournament of Church *versus* State, and the sympathies of the onlooker usually sided with his representative. The wrestlers stripped stark in the tents right and left of the *gegen*'s—the lamas in one and the "black men" in the other—and drew on a stout pair of cotton drawers and a curious garment consisting of back and sleeves only, and many of them kept on their long leather boots, adding a casing of felt to protect the shins. Kicking was in order, and most of the wrestling was a mere exhibition of force, but now and then a dextrous trick showed long practice or great quickness. One lama attracted attention by his physical development and the evident superiority of his "science"; he threw his antagonist, a huge yamên clerk, at once by a lightning dart at a foot which he jerked up. But in the majority of cases the bout began by an orthodox grip, neck to neck and shoulder to shoulder, and ended by a trip or a violent throw.

The comical feature of the contests was the preliminary challenge. Each, as he emerged from the dressing tent and came in sight of the *gegen*, brought himself by a series of standing jumps to the pavilion, sprang as high in the air as he could, bowed low with a smack of the hands to the ground, followed this by a couple of high springs, turned round and leaped into a minatory [threatening] position in the centre of the plot, where he waited until his adversary had accomplished a similar performance. The beaten candidate usually took his ill-fortune with good grace, though his friends rarely failed to greet his fall with loud and appropriate sarcasm, and retired to the dressing tent; but the victor, by a fresh series of leaps, accompanied by whoops, presented himself once more to the *gegen*, prostrated himself, was invested with his hat, and given a double-handful of cheese scraps, which he partly ate and partly scattered amongst the onlookers. The tournament lasts till sundown and usually ends in an easy victory for the Church, the lamas being by far the greater adepts.

## CHARACTERISTIC FAUNA

The fauna of East Mongolia, though characteristic, is not remarkable. The only beast of special interest to the sportsman is the *kures*, the *huang-yang* of the Chinese (*Antilope guttirosa*), which is found everywhere from Chaharia to the Kerulon. It is assiduously hunted by the Mongols, and consequently wary and difficult of approach. In the sandhills of Geshikten, roedeer (*Cervus pygargus*) existed in small number, and nearing the Kentei Mountains I heard of elk and saw some horns, which were purchased by Chinese traders as medicine. This elk was called *hantehai* by the traders, and one gathers from the pages of Du Halde that they had a wider range in Mongolia two centuries ago than they have now. Gerbillon mentions the killing of a wild horse (*Equus hemionus*) some 25 miles south of the Kerulon in 1689, and Radde 50 years ago procured some specimens in the region north of Lake Kulun, but none of the Mongols I met knew of such a beast, and he probably no longer exists in East Mongolia.

In Chaharia the burrows of the suslik (*Spermolegus mongolicus*), the "Pharaoh's rat" of Polo no doubt, are innumerable; a marmot, called *tarbukh* (*Arctomys bobac*) takes his place in the more hilly regions of Uchimuchin and the Khalha Khanates, and the flesh and fur are sufficiently esteemed to attract constant pursuit. Near Angul Nor I shot a small jerboa (*Dipus annulatus*), and was informed that he was fairly common. Wolves are of frequent occurrence, especially in

North Mongolia; foxes (*Canis corsac*), raccoon dogs (*Canis procyonoides*), hares (*Lepus tolai*), badgers, moles, and hedgehogs are numerous; colonies of hamsters and field mice abound.

Pallas' sand grouse (*Syrrhaptes paradoxus*) was met with all along our route, but chiefly in the Kerulon Valley, where the flocks were numerous and large; the grey partridges nested in small numbers in Geshikten and Uchimuchin; the quail (*Coturnix japonicus*) was flushed everywhere; and scarce a week passed in which it was not possible to keep the larder supplied with bustard (*Otis tarda*). Eagles, ospreys, hawks, kites, or harriers were seen daily, and owls occasionally. The house swallow (*H. gutturalis*) is found in every temple and in many tents; a tiny board is slung specially under the smoke hole for his reception, and care is taken to avoid injuring nest or young, the presence of a swallow in a tent being considered very auspicious. Sand martins and swifts are occasionally seen, and the hoopoe nests in stacks of argol [dung used as fuel] in Chaharia.

On the Khalha River warblers, willow-wrens, and shrikes were first noticed in number. Ravens made themselves obnoxious to the camels, especially in the neighbourhood of Urga; Daurian jackdaws flocked in many valleys of Chaharia and Uchimuchin; rooks congregated in all populous places, and I noticed that red-billed choughs (*Fregilus graculus*) took the place of crows at most monasteries and in the town of Dolonnor. Cuckoos were calling incessantly in the sand-hills of Geshikten, and the note of the Mongol lark

(*Melanocorypha mongolica*), one of the most remarkable of song birds, was heard from Kalgan to the Kerulon. Sparrows flourished around all habitations, and in the Kerulon Valley I came across tits (*Parus minor*), who infested the felt tents as fearlessly as the sparrows. Chats (*Saxicola ænanthe*), wagtails, starlings, buntings (*Euspiza aureola, Emberiza spodocephala, E. elegans, Epusilla* were most frequent), and pipits were common. Of water and marsh birds the number was legion: cranes (*Grus cinerea* and *G. leucanchen*), lapwing, plovers, sandpipers, godwits, snipe, herons, rails, coots, swans, geese, and ducks innumerable, cormorants, terns, and gulls. It was rare to see a pond without its pair of sheldrakes (*Casarca rutila* or *Tadorna cornuta*), and a family of young ones.

I saw few species of reptiles; tiny lizards, an occasional non-venomous snake, frogs, and toads. But wherever there was any luxuriance of vegetation mosquitoes, gnats, and flies swarmed in force, and caused some misery to man and beast; and colonies of ants and spiders infested the most arid places.

## MONGOLIAN TRADE

I think I can best describe the character of Mongolian trade by sketching the operations of a firm at whose place of business on the Upper Kerulon I spent a couple of nights. The house of Lin Sheng Yüan has existed for nearly 200 years, ever since the foundation of the Mai-mai-chên of Urga. Their trade is the usual one in these parts—bartering miscellaneous goods (copper vessels, Russian leather boots, hats and caps, drills, cottons, satins, embroidery, silk and woollen braid, Japanese looking-glasses, snuff-bottles, cane whip-handles, Chinese stirrups, bridles and saddles, tobacco pouches, flint and steel, pipes, incense, Japanese matches, artificial flowers, fans, bows and arrows; also oat and wheat flour, parched millet, dried jujubes, Russian loaf sugar, sugar candy, Chinese spirits and tea) for cattle, ponies, felt, hides, timber, and deerhorn. There were 30 Chinese employees, all Shansi men, who spoke a lamentable Mongol, and they were spread over eight stations in the valleys of the Tola, Khara, and Upper Kerulon. Not one of these men made his home in Mongolia, and all were given in turn a year's leave to Shansi after two of service. The men departing on leave took with them the season's collection of hides, etc., which was carried across the Gobi, deposited with the firm's branch at Kalgan, and then disposed of to agents of wholesale houses from the large cities of North China. The building I stayed at was protected by a stout palisade of larch poles 10 feet high, within which a few fierce Mongol watch-dogs were let loose nightly, much to my discomfort, for they made no distinction between mere guests and strangers. Inside the stockade were the living rooms and offices, stores and stables, of the usual Chinese type, and a tiny vegetable garden in which onions, garlic, and Shantung cabbage were grown. Outside there was a number of small warehouses—log huts for the storage of the less important articles, and a huge pile of cut logs for fuel.

They are close traders, these Shansi men; soft of speech, yet tenacious. A Russian friend described to me from actual experience their method of exploiting the Mongol. In matters of dress and ornament the nomad is like a child; whatever he sees he wants. The Chinese trade on this foible. A Mongol sees a robe which he admires in a Shansi trader's tent; he is a man of small means, without ready money or spare cattle to pay for such an article. The Chinaman, who knows his circumstances exactly, gives him the robe, remarking that he can pay for it some other time. Nothing is said for a year perhaps, when the Chinaman will drop casually into the Mongol's tent in the most friendly manner and in the course of conversation refers to the robe. The Mongol is surprised at the price put upon it and of course cannot pay it. The Chinese is not in the least put out, suggests amicably that something might be given on account, and succeeds in carrying away some animal or article of value to him which he registers to the man's credit. The horse or sheep, or whatever it is, is probably worth the robe, but it only appears in the account as an abatement of interest, which is reckoned by the month and is of course compound.

This goes on for some seasons, and after a few years the Mongol becomes alive to the fact that the robe (by this time the debt has probably been increased by other and similar items) keeps him in grinding poverty. He pays the Chinese most of his surplus stock every year, and yet finds that he is deeper in debt than ever. The full bearing of this fact

is concealed from him by the politeness of the
Chinese who never presses the bill too stiffly: his
object is to keep the debt going, and so long as he gets
an animal or two a year his dividend is handsome. The
book-keeping is voluminous, and there is a tremendous amount of elaborate dunning [debt-collecting]
to be accomplished, but these are fascinating pursuits
to the Shansi trader, and in Mongolia they appear to
take the place of ordinary recreation. There is no class
of European trader who can attempt to compete with
these Shansi men in the intricate and patient bartering which is so necessary in dealing with Mongols.

Representatives of such firms as Lin Sheng Yüan
itinerate all over East Mongolia during the summer
and autumn, and are to be found for limited periods
at important monasteries and in populous neighbour-
hoods. They hail from Peking, Kalgan, Dolon-nor,
Kuei-hua-ch'êng, Urga, and Khailar. I came across the
tents of a Peking dealer north of the Bur Nor, and
caravans of Dolon-nor and Kalgan men were seen in
numbers along the Kerulon. Chinese hucksters, with
a bull-cart escorted by a fierce dog, abounded
throughout the Chahar country and Inner Mongolia;
they sold flour, salt, parched millet, and spirits for
hides, sheepskins, and wool. Their profits, at the best
nothing great, were enhanced by doctored balances. I
found the price of a catty [1⅓ lbs] of flour on the
Khalha River exactly double that of Dolon-nor, and
millet cost three times as much; moreover, the catty
fell from the normal 1⅓ lbs to 1⅒ lbs, and the tael of
silver was 8 per cent heavier than that of Kalgan.

Silver, generally of inferior quality, is the recognized currency everywhere, but the Russian rouble notes are making great headway in Urga and Kerulon Valley. My cheques on the Hong Kong and Shanghai Bank at Peking were accepted by Chinese traders at Sambeise Urgo, none of whom knew me personally, and a Mongol lama, from whom I purchased a pony near Kulun Nor, preferred a draft on the Russo-Chinese Bank at Urga to some inferior silver which constituted my last reserve of hard cash. This readiness to accept paper money is due to the vogue of the Russian credit rouble and to the great reputation of these two well-known banks. As a minor currency, and for all small purchases, bricks of tea are much used everywhere: I saw that they were accepted instead of small silver across the counter of the Russo-Chinese Bank at Urga.

# PRÉCIS OF PRINCIPAL EVENTS IN THE HISTORY OF RUSSIAN INTERCOURSE AND TRAVEL IN NORTH AND EAST MONGOLIA

*(From Bretschneider and other sources)*

## AD 1619–1700

According to old official records preserved in Siberia, the beginning of Russian intercourse with China dates from 1619–1620. In one or other of these years the Voivod of Tobolsk, Kuryakin, sent two Cossacks (Petlin and Kiselev) to open communications with the Chinese Court.

They set out from Tomsk, which had been founded 15 or 16 years previously, and passed through the whole of Mongolia from north-west to south-east to Kalgan, and thence to Peking, which they called the "White City".

The Tushetu Khan of the Khalhas sent a fowling-piece and other articles "to Russia": the Tsetsen Khan also. Both are referred to as "tribute" in the "Shuo Fang Pei Ch'êng Piao". The name O-lo-ssŭ (Russia) seems to have been first heard in China in 1639.

A mission, dispatched by the Tsar Alexis under the leadership of Baikov, entered Mongolia by the valley of the Black Irtish, journeyed along the foot of the South Altai, and across the Gobi to Kuei-hua-ch'êng, Kalgan, and Peking.

Baikov appears to have been received with sufficient courtesy at Peking, but his troubles began when he refused to perform the ceremonial required of him by Chinese etiquette. He yielded a point in surrendering his presents before seeing the Emperor, but he flatly refused to give up a letter of the Tsar into any hands but the Emperor's, and also declined to exhibit the letter to the Chinese officials whose duty it was to examine such documents before presentation. After five months of waiting he was again asked to appear before the Tribunal to explain his method of saluting the Emperor, he having said that he would render the same tokens of respect which he would pay to his own Sovereign. He refused point blank. The presents were returned immediately with a homily on his bad manners and presumption in asking for privileges which a predecessor, Yavishin, had done without. Baikov accordingly left Peking (4th September, 1655). Before he reached Kalgan he sent a messenger back to say that he would yield on all the points desired by the Chinese—he would not insist on seeing the Emperor, and would conform to the etiquette of the Chinese Court—and continued his march for three days in Mongolia. This continuation of his march was considered another proof of bad manners, and on it was based his final dismissal.

*Toutes les façons d'agir accusent chez toi une complète ignorance dans l'art de savoir maintenir la dignité Souveraine.* [All your actions show a complete ignorance of the art of respecting sovereign dignity.]

Baikov returned the way he came, and reached Tobolsk on the 31st July, 1656. His route was the ordinary one followed by Kalmucks and others at this period, and it was taken again by Perfiliev in 1659.

The founding of Nertchinsk in Dauria (so called from a Tungus people, the *Dahuri*) in 1658, and of Selenginsk in 1666, shifted the route to China. Both these places furnished a nearer basis for intercourse with Peking. A trade caravan led by Milovanov in 1670 was the first to essay the route from Nertchinsk via Tsuruhaitu, Khailar, the Hingan range, Tsitsihar, and Hsi-fêng-k'ou to Peking. Spafary followed the same route in 1675.

The route to Peking via Kiakhta had been known to the Russians ever since the founding of Selenginsk in 1666.

In 1674 Porshennikov crossed the Gobi with a trading caravan, and was the pioneer of the Kiakhta–Kalgan route; but it was not the recognized trade route until after the conclusion of the Burinsky Treaty (so named after the River Bura) in 1727.

Venyukov and Favorov sent to Peking with Imperial credentials by the Kiakhta route [1686].

Treaty of Nertchinsk fixing the boundary between East Siberia and the Chinese dominions [1689].

Isbrant Ides reached Peking by almost the same route as Spafary [1693].

## 1700–1800

Lorenz Lange was sent to Peking by Peter the Great. The primary objects of this mission were to learn about Chinese architecture and art for use in the construction of the Peterhof Palace, and to make special observations on the trade and condition of the Siberian frontier. With Lange went Thomas Garvin, an English physician. Lange and Garvin left Selenginsk in October 1716 and reached Peking in November.

Peter the Great was so pleased with the results of Lange's mission that he sent Ismailov as Ambassador Extraordinary in 1720. Lange went with Ismailov as Secretary, and was appointed Peter's agent to reside in

Peking. John Bell, of Antermony, was a member of the Ismailov mission.

Ismailov did not succeed in negotiating a Treaty, and he returned to Russia in 1721, leaving Lange behind him. Complications on the Siberian frontier made the Chinese unfriendly to Lange, and he left in June 1722.

The botanist Messerschmidt travelled extensively in Siberia in the period of 1720–1727, under the auspices of Peter the Great. In 1724 he visited the Dalai Nor of North-East Mongolia.

Another envoy, Vladislavich, was sent to Peking in 1726. He was accompanied by Lange. Returning to the Siberian frontier the mission reached the River Bura, and in August 1727 concluded the so-called Burinsky Treaty. From here Lange was again dispatched to Peking, where he remained until July 1728. Kiakhta was founded in consequence of the Treaty and the Kiakhta route became the most favoured by caravans across Mongolia.

Lange set out from Kiakhta in November 1731 with a caravan, but did not reach Peking till March 1732; the hardships of this winter journey induced him to return by the old Manchurian route via Hsi-fêng-k'ou, Tsitsihar, and Tsuruhaitu.

Lange made his sixth and last journey to Peking in 1736–1737 by the Manchurian route; he returned by the Kiakhta route.

After Lange three official Russian trade caravans went to Peking in 1741, 1745, and 1754. The Russian Government finding these caravans unprofitable discontinued them after 1754. Up to this time the

Decennial Ecclesiastical Missions provided for by the Burinsky Treaty usually accompanied the trade caravans, but now they were sent specially.

## 1800–1900

The next great Russian mission to China was that of Count Golovkin, with whom went the ninth Ecclesiastical Mission and a remarkable scientific staff under Count Pototski, including the celebrated Klaproth. Golovkin was kept three months at Kiakhta waiting for the Chinese to make up their minds whether they would receive him; part of the mission got as far as Urga in 1805, but permission to continue the journey was refused by the Chinese Government and it returned to Kiakhta in January 1806. The ninth Decennial Mission did not leave Kiakhta for Peking until September 1807.

Tenth Ecclesiastical Mission under Timkovski [1820–1821].

Eleventh Ecclesiastical Mission under Ladizhenski. The astronomer Fuss and the botanist Bunge accompanied it [1830–1831].

Twelfth Ecclesiastical Mission. Dr Tatarinov accompanied this mission [1840].

Thirteenth Decennial Mission under Colonel Kovalevski [1849].

The route from Kiakhta to Peking was sketched (flying survey) by Volkov [1858].

General Ignatiev crossed the Gobi to Peking; his route was sketched by Shimkovich [1859].

The Russian Treaty with China, concluded at Peking in 1860, secured the right to trade at Kalgan and Urga and to station Consuls at Urga and Kashgar. The Russian postal service across the Gobi from Kiakhta to Peking, which still exists, was also established under this Treaty.

Dr Fritsche, physician at the Russian Legation at Peking, made a series of journeys in Mongolia between 1868 and 1877; one in Inner Mongolia, another from Hei-shui via Pai-ta-tzu to Khailar and Tsuruhaitu, and two by different routes between Kiakhta and Kalgan.

The well-known travels of Przhvalski began in this year [1870].

The Butin brothers, merchants of Nertchinsk, passed south from the Khulustai guard-house through the mid-Kerulon to Dolon-nor in 1870. They were accompanied by the botanist Lomonosov.

Travels of Pevtsov, chiefly in West Mongolia. (Pevtsov first appears in Mongolia as Captain of the Cossack guard sent to convoy a supply of corn which was furnished by Russian merchants to the Chinese troops under Tso Tsung-t'ang engaged in the suppression of Yakub Bey.) [1878–1879].

Vanin, a Russian topographer, travelled from Dolon-nor to Urga [1882]. Lieutenant Evtyugin followed the same route as the Butins through the Middle Kerulon to Dolon-nor, returning to Siberia by the caravan route through Khailar.

Colonel Harnack, of the Russian General Staff, examined the Khingan Mountains in the summer of 1887.

Colonel Putiata, Russian military agent in China, explored the South Khingan Mountains in 1891.

Travels of Pozdnyéev. (M. Pozdnyéev, formerly Professor of the Mongol language at the University of St Petersburgh, and now Director of the School of Oriental Languages at Vladivostock, has travelled extensively along the caravan routes all over Mongolia, but his longest continuous journeys were made in 1892–1893.)

Journey of Colonel Strelbitski (Russian General Staff) in the valley of the Kerulon [1894]. The itinerary of this journey has not been published.

Klementz visited Djun Khure and the Upper Kerulon. (Klementz, a well-known Siberian archaeologist, has travelled extensively in West Mongolia.)

Potanin journeyed eastward from Bur Nor (Buir or Buyur Nor) into the Aru-Khorchin country [1899]. (There is no living traveller who has seen so much of Mongolia and the Mongol-Chinese borderlands as Potanin. In Mongolia his principal journeys have been in the north-west.)

An expedition under Dr Damaskin, to investigate the spread of bubonic plague in East Mongolia and North China, travelled along the Kerulon from Urga to Ganjur Sume, and thence passed south-eastward into the trans-Khingan region [1899].

*Note.* The Mongolian frontier on the north remains to this day as it was fixed by the Treaties of 1689 and 1727. Until the middle of the nineteenth century the Amur was not yet the dividing line between Chinese

Manchuria and East Siberia, and Russia had no coast outlet south of 55° north latitude. There were two harbours, Okhotsk and Ayan, but they were too far north to be accessible during a great part of the year. Petropavlosk in Kamschatka, it is true, is in 53° north latitude, and more generally accessible, but its distance from the more favoured regions of Siberia and the Amur valley kept it in the background. It was plainly unsuitable, and as there were many harbours to the south situated much more favourably, to the possession of which the Chinese appeared to attach no importance whatever, it was not strange that the Russians turned their attention southward to secure the great want—an ice-free port in a decently accessible position, which could form an eastern outlet for the vast Siberian territory.

In the early half of the nineteenth century the geography of this part of the Asiatic coast was little known. Neither La Perouse (1787) nor Krusenstern (1805) had ascertained that Sagalien was an island, and the mouth of the Amur still remained undiscovered. In 1847 General Muravieff, who had made a reputation in the Caucasus, was entrusted with the Governorship of East Siberia, and from that time events began to move. The mouth of the Amur was discovered in June 1849, and the existence of the narrow passage between Sagalien and the mainland, which gives access to the Amur from the south, was established. In 1850 a Russo-American Trading Company (the Hudson's Bay Company of these regions) founded a station called *Petrovskoye Zimoviye*

(Peter's winter quarters) on the Sea of Okhotsk, and in 1851 Nikolayevsk was founded. In 1853 De Castries Bay (named by La Perouse after the then French Minister of Marine) was occupied and the military post, Alexandrovsk, founded; also Barracouta Bay, where Constantinovsk was established. A post of 150 men was placed on the south of Sagalien and another was established at Marinsk. Muravieff steamed down the Shilka and Amur in 1854 on board the *Argun*, a small steamer which had been built at a foundry established on the Shilka—and this demonstrated the navigability of the great waterway of North-East Asia.

All this time Russia had been invading and occupying Chinese territory without any regard to the rights of the owners, and the Chinese Government was, of course, very much exercised by these unneighbourly proceedings. In 1857 Admiral Putiatin was entrusted with a diplomatic mission to regularize the Russian occupations in Manchurian territory, but did not succeed. Muravieff, however, accomplished the task by the Treaty of Aigun, concluded with Chinese Plenipotentiaries who were sent to the Amur for the purpose. The task was, of course, facilitated by the hostilities with France and England, and in 1860 General Ignatieff took advantage of the fresh complications to secure all the country east of the Ussuri River, thus bringing the Russian coastline down to the Korean border, where it remains at present.

# Other titles in the series

## The Amritsar Massacre: General Dyer in the Punjab, 1919

*"We feel that General Dyer, by adopting an inhuman and un-British method of dealing with subjects of His Majesty the King-Emperor, has done great disservice to the interest of British rule in India. This aspect it was not possible for the people of the mentality of General Dyer to realise."*

*Backdrop*

At the time of the events described, India was under British rule. Indians had fought alongside the British in World War I, and had made tremendous financial contributions to the British war effort. Mahatma Gandhi was the leader of the Indian National Congress party, which was seeking independence from the British Empire.

*The Book*

This is the story of the action taken by Brigadier-General Dyer at Amritsar in the Punjab in 1919. Faced with insurrection in support of Mahatma Gandhi, the British Army attempted to restore order. General Dyer, on arriving in the troubled city of Amritsar, issued an order banning any assembly of more than four people. Consequently, when he discovered a large crowd gathered together during a cattle fair, he took the astonishing action of shooting more than three hundred unarmed people. Regarding the subsequent native obedience as a satisfactory result, he was surprised to find himself removed from command a year later, and made lengthy representations to Parliament.

ISBN 0 11 702412 0          Price £6.99

# British Battles of World War I, 1914–15

*"The effect of these poisonous gases was so virulent as to render the whole of the line held by the French Division incapable of any action at all. It was at first impossible for anyone to realise what had actually happened. The smoke and fumes hid everything from sight, and hundreds of men were thrown into a comatose or dying condition, and within an hour the whole position had to be abandoned, together with about 50 guns."*

*Backdrop*
On 4 August 1914, Britain declared war on Germany. Germany had already invaded Belgium and France and was progressing towards Paris.

*The Book*
These are the despatches from some of the battles of the first two years of World War I. They include action in northern France, Germany, Gallipoli, and even as far afield as the Cocos Islands in the Indian Ocean. They describe the events of battle, the tremendous courage, the huge losses, and the confusions and difficulties of war. These startling accounts, which were written by the generals at the front, were first published in the "London Gazette", the official newspaper of Parliament.

ISBN  0 11 702447 3          Price  £6.99

## Florence Nightingale and the Crimea, 1854–55

*"By an oversight, no candles were included among the stores brought to the Crimea. Lamps and wicks were brought but not oil. These omissions were not supplied until after possession had been taken of Balaklava, and the purveyor had an opportunity of purchasing candles and oil from the shipping and the dealers in the town."*

### Backdrop

The British Army arrived in the Crimea in 1854, ill-equipped to fight a war in the depths of a Russian winter.

### The Book

The hospital service for wounded soldiers during the Crimean War was very poor and became the subject of concern, not just in the army, but also in the press. "The Times" was publishing letters from the families of soldiers describing the appalling conditions. This embarrassed the government, but even more it irritated the army, which did not know how to cope with such open scrutiny of its activities.

The book is a collection of extracts from government papers published in 1855 and 1856. Their selection provides a snapshot of events at that time. In particular they focus on the terrible disaster that was the Charge of the Light Brigade, and the inadequate provisions that were made for the care of the sick and wounded. The documents relating to the hospitals at Scutari include evidence from Florence Nightingale herself.

ISBN  0 11 702425 2        Price  £6.99

# Lord Kitchener and Winston Churchill: The Dardanelles Commission Part I, 1914–15

*"The naval attack on the Narrows was never resumed. It is difficult to understand why the War Council did not meet between 19th March and 14th May. The failure of the naval attack showed the necessity of abandoning the plan of forcing the passage of the Dardanelles by purely naval operation. The War Council should then have met and considered the future policy to be pursued."*

## Backdrop

The Dardanelles formed part of the main southern shipping route to Russia, and was of great military and strategic importance. However, it had long been recognised by the British naval and military authorities that any attack on the Dardanelles would be an operation fraught with great difficulties.

## The Book

During the early stages of World War I, Russia made a plea to her allies to make a demonstration against the Turks. So attractive was the prize of the Dardanelles to the British generals, notably Lord Kitchener, that this ill-fated campaign was launched. Just how powerful an influence Kitchener was to exert over the War Council, and just how ill-prepared the Allies were to conduct such an attack, are revealed in dramatic detail in the report of this Commission.

The book covers the first part of the Commission's report. It deals with the origin, inception and conduct of operations in the Dardanelles from the beginning of the war in August 1914 until March 1915, when the idea of a purely naval attack was abandoned.

ISBN  0 11 702423 6         Price  £6.99

# The Russian Revolution, 1917

*"It is the general opinion in Ekaterinburg that the Empress, her son, and four daughters were not murdered, but were despatched on the 17th July to the north or the west. The story that they were burnt in a house seems to be an exaggeration of the fact that in a wood outside the town was found a heap of ashes, apparently the result of burning a considerable amount of clothing. At the bottom of the ashes was a diamond, and, as one of the Grand Duchesses is said to have sewn a diamond into the lining of her cloak, it is supposed that the clothes of the Imperial family were burnt there."*

### Backdrop

By November 1917 Russia had lost more than twenty million people in the war. Lenin's Bolshevik party had overthrown the Tsar and had called for an end to all capitalist governments.

### The Book

Government files contain a number of detailed documents describing the nature of the Bolshevik Revolution and the government of Lenin, which was observed to be not only abhorrent but also menacing because of the international implications. The book is compiled from two of these files, one of which describes the events leading up to the revolution and how the Bolsheviks came to power in October 1917. The other contains a series of eye-witness accounts of the frightening days of the Bolshevik regime from the summer of 1918 to April 1919.

ISBN 0 11 702424 4        Price £6.99

# UFOs in the House of Lords, 1979

*"Is it not time that Her Majesty's Government informed our people of what they know about UFOs? The UFOs have been coming in increasing numbers for 30 years since the war, and I think it is time our people were told the truth. We have not been invaded from outer space. Most incidents have not been hostile. Indeed it is us, the earthlings, who have fired on them. . . . Whatever the truth is, I am sure that an informed public is a prepared one. Another thing: it is on record that both sighting and landing reports are increasing all the time. Just suppose the 'ufonauts' decided to make mass landings tomorrow in this country—there could well be panic here, because our people have not been prepared."*

### Backdrop

The winter of 1978/79 in Britain was a time of strikes and unrest. It became known as the "winter of discontent". Yet it seems that the House of Lords had other more important things to discuss.

### The Book

The book is the transcript of a debate in the House of Lords which took place in February 1979. Their Lordships debated the need for an international initiative in response to the problem of Unidentified Flying Objects. There were several notable speeches from noble lords and distinguished prelates.

ISBN  0 11 702413 9              Price  £6.99

# D Day to VE Day: General Eisenhower's Report, 1944–45

*"During the spring of 1945, as the sky grew darker over Germany, the Nazi leaders had struggled desperately, by every means in their power, to whip their people into a last supreme effort to stave off defeat, hoping against hope that it would be possible, if only they could hold out long enough, to save the day by dividing the Allies. Blinded as they were by their own terror and hatred of 'Bolshevism', they were incapable of understanding the strength of the bond of common interest existing between Britain, the United States and the Soviet Union."*

*Backdrop*

In 1944 the Allies were poised to launch an attack against Hitler's German war machine. The planning and timing were crucial. In February, General Eisenhower was appointed Supreme Commander of the Allied Operations in Europe.

*The Book*

The book is Dwight D. Eisenhower's personal account of the Allied invasion of Europe, from the preparations for the D-Day landings in Normandy, France, to the final assault across Germany. He presents a story of a far more arduous struggle than is commonly portrayed against an enemy whose tenacity he admired and whose skills he feared. It is a tactical account of his understanding of enemy manoeuvres, and his attempts to counter their actions. The formality of the report is coloured by many personal touches, and the reader senses Eisenhower's growing determination to complete the task. Hindsight would have had the general take more notice of Russian activity, but that this was not obvious to him is one of the fascinations of such a contemporary document.

ISBN  0 11 702451 1          Price  £6.99

# The Irish Uprising, 1914-21: Papers from the British Parliamentary Archive

*"Captain Bowen-Colthurst adopted the extraordinary, and indeed almost meaningless, course of taking Mr Sheehy Skeffington with him as a 'hostage'. He had no right to take Mr Sheehy Skeffington out of the custody of the guard for this or any other purpose, and he asked no one's leave to do so. . . . Before they left the barracks Mr Sheehy Skeffington's hands were tied behind his back and Captain Bowen-Colthurst called upon him to say his prayers. Upon Mr Sheehy Skeffington refusing to do so Captain Bowen-Colthurst ordered the men of his party to take their hats off and himself uttered a prayer, the words of it being: 'O Lord God, if it shall please thee to take away the life of this man forgive him for Christ's sake.'"*

### Backdrop
In 1914 it was still the case that the whole of Ireland was part of Great Britain, under the dominion of the King, and Irish constituencies were represented in the British Parliament.

### The Book
This book contains five remarkable documents published by the British Government between 1914 and 1921, relating to the events leading up to the partition of Ireland in 1921. In the first, a report is made into the shooting of civilians following a landing of arms at Howth outside Dublin. The second is of the papers discovered relating to the activities of Sinn Fein and particularly of Sir Roger Casement. The third is the government inquiry into the Easter Rising of 1916. The fourth describes the treatment of three journalists by the British Army shortly after the uprising, and the last is an exchange of correspondence between Eamon de Valera and David Lloyd George prior to the Anglo-Irish Treaty of 1921.

ISBN  0 11 702415 5         Price  £6.99

# The Siege of the Peking Embassy, 1900

*"I cannot conclude this despatch without saying a word of praise respecting the ladies of all nationalities who so ably and devotedly assisted the defence, notwithstanding the terrible shadow which at all times hung over the legation—a shadow which the never-ceasing rattle of musketry and crash of round shot and shell and the diminishing number of defenders rendered ever present. They behaved with infinite patience and cheerfulness, helping personally in the hospital or, in making sandbags and bandages, and in assisting in every possible way the work of defence. Especially commended are two young ladies—Miss Myers and Miss Daisy Brazier—who daily filtered the water for the hospital, in tropical heat, and carried it with bullets whistling and shells bursting in the trees overhead."* Sir Claude MacDonald

*Backdrop*
The Boxer movement in China was a secret society which preached hatred of foreigners. By the spring of 1900, this movement was out of control. On 9 June, the Boxers launched their first attack against foreign property in Peking by burning down the racecourse. On 19 June, all foreigners were order to evacuate Peking within 24 hours. The order was not complied with.

*The Book*
As events worsened for the diplomats and their families in Peking, Sir Claude MacDonald, the British ambassador, wired the Admiralty in Taku to request the immediate despatch of a relief force. Just how that relief force fared, and how the hundreds of diplomats and their families who were stranded inside the Legation buildings coped with the rigours of the siege, are the subject of the diplomatic papers presented in this book. The central part of the story is the gripping diary of events kept by Sir Claude MacDonald.

ISBN 0 11 702456 2 Price £6.99

# The Siege of Kars, 1855

*"We had, up to that date, suffered from cold, want of sufficient clothing, and starvation, without a murmur escaping from the troops. They fell dead at their posts, in their tents, and throughout the camp as brave men should who cling to their duty through the slightest glimmering of hope of saving a place entrusted to their custody. From the day of their glorious victory on 29th September, they had not tasted animal food, and their nourishment consisted of two-fifths of a ration of bread and the roots of grass, which they scarcely had the strength to dig for; yet night and day they stood to their arms, their wasted frames showing the fearful effects of starvation, but their sparkling eye telling me what they would do were the enemy to attack them again."* W. F. Williams

*Backdrop*

In 1855, while the British Army was fighting alongside the French and the Turkish armies in the Crimean War, a little-known but serious siege was taking place in the city of Kars in eastern Turkey. Set within mountains and overlooking a gorge, Kars is a natural fortress, but its possession by the Turks was threatened by the Russians.

*The Book*

During the Crimean War, the British were giving aid to the Turkish army by lending them generals to help organise and strengthen their garrisons. General Williams had arrived in Kars in September 1854, having been appointed British Military Commissioner with the Turkish Army in Asia. He soon began organising the troops there, although his repeated requests for supplies and reinforcements were met with delay and obfuscation. These despatches concerning the siege of Kars date from May 1855. Their unfolding tells a sorry tale of heroism and frustrated hope.

ISBN 0 11 702454 6               Price £6.99

# *Defeat at Gallipoli: The Dardanelles Commission Part II, 1915–16*

> *"It has been represented ... that from a military point of view, the Dardanelles Expedition, even if unsuccessful, was justified by the fact that it neutralised or contained a large number of Turkish troops who otherwise would have been free to operate elsewhere. Lord Kitchener estimated this number as being nearly 300,000. But in containing the Turkish force, we employed ... a total of at least 400,000. Our casualties amounted to 31,389 killed, 78,749 wounded and 9,708 missing, making a total of 119,846. The expedition also involved heavy financial expenditure and the employment of a considerable naval force."*

### Backdrop

The naval attempt by the British to force the Dardanelles was abandoned in March 1915. Rather than losing face, the military commanders decided to send a large army to the area.

### The Book

Picking up the story from where the earlier volume, *Lord Kitchener and Winston Churchill*, left off, this second part of the Dardanelles Commission's report deals with the disastrous military campaign to capture the Gallipoli Peninsula using ground forces. As the story unfolds, we learn how the Allies were unable to make any headway against an enemy who was well prepared and well positioned. Within a few months the Allies had suffered a humiliating defeat, and thousands of men had lost their lives. The realisation of the government's incompetence in handling this affair was instrumental in the removal of Herbert Asquith as Prime Minister in December 1916.

ISBN  0 11 702455 4          Price  £6.99

# The Strange Story of Adolph Beck

*"He said he was Lord Winton de Willoughby. He asked why I lived alone in a flat. I said I had an income and wished to do so . . . Two or three hours after he had gone I missed some tigers' claws and the teeth of an animal mounted in silver with my monogram."*

*Backdrop*

The foggy streets of Edwardian London were alive with cads, swindlers, ladies of dubious reputation and all manner of low life who fed on human frailty.

*The Book*

In 1895, Adolph Beck was arrested and convicted of the crimes of deception and larceny. Using the alias Lord Winton de Willoughby, he had entered into the apartments of several ladies, some of whom preferred, for obvious reasons, not to give their names. The ladies gave evidence, as did a handwriting expert, and Mr Beck was imprisoned. But an utterly bizarre sequence of events culminated in a judge who declared that, since he could himself determine perfectly whether the accused was of the criminal classes or not, juries should never be allowed to decide the outcome of a trial. The account given here is of one of the strangest true stories in the entire British legal history.

ISBN  0 11 7024147          Price  £6.99

# *Wilfrid Blunt's Egyptian Garden:*
# *Fox Hunting in Cairo*

*"Cairo. July 23, 1901 – On Sunday morning a fox-hunt was taking place near Cairo, in the desert, the hounds following a scent crossed the boundary-wall of Mr. Wilfrid Blunt's property, and two of the field, being British officers, who were acting as whips, went in to turn them back. Mr. Blunt's watchmen surrounded them, and, although they explained their intention, treated them with considerable violence."*

### Backdrop

In the days of Empire, the British way of life was carried on with a blithe disregard for local peculiarities and this went hand in hand with a sometimes benevolent, sometimes despotic, belief in the innate inferiority of those under its thumb.

### The Book

In 1900, the Imperial British Army occupied Egypt and, in order to provide sport for the officers who were kicking their heels, a pack of hounds was shipped out from England to hunt the Egyptian fox. Unfortunately, the desert provides poor cover and, one day, the pack followed in hot pursuit by the officers, found itself in the garden of the rich and eccentric poet Wilfrid Scarwen Blunt. Attempting to protect the absent Mr. Blunt's property, his servants tried to prevent the hunt and were promptly arrested. Mr. Blunt objected to the officers' behaviour, both to the government and the press, and the matter became quite a scandal.

ISBN  0 11 702416 3                    Price  £6.99